Markus Modzelewski

Inclusive design for early phases of product development process

Markus Modzelewski

# Inclusive design for early phases of product development process

Südwestdeutscher Verlag für Hochschulschriften

**Impressum / Imprint**

Bibliografische Information der Deutschen Nationalbibliothek: Die Deutsche Nationalbibliothek verzeichnet diese Publikation in der Deutschen Nationalbibliografie; detaillierte bibliografische Daten sind im Internet über http://dnb.d-nb.de abrufbar.

Bibliographic information published by the Deutsche Nationalbibliothek: The Deutsche Nationalbibliothek lists this publication in the Deutsche Nationalbibliografie; detailed bibliographic data are available in the Internet at http://dnb.d-nb.de.

Coverbild / Cover image: www.ingimage.com

Verlag / Publisher:
Südwestdeutscher Verlag für Hochschulschriften
ist ein Imprint der / is a trademark of
OmniScriptum GmbH & Co. KG
Heinrich-Böcking-Str. 6-8, 66121 Saarbrücken, Deutschland / Germany
Email: info@svh-verlag.de

Herstellung: siehe letzte Seite /
Printed at: see last page
**ISBN: 978-3-8381-5066-6**

Zugl. / Approved by: Bremen, Universität, Diss., 2014

"If you can't explain it simply, you don't understand it well enough." - Albert Einstein

# Acknowledgements

First of all, I would like to thank my advisor Prof. Dr. Michael Lawo for motivating and supporting me during my work. This thesis would not be possible without him.

I would also like to thank Dr. Patrick Langdon as my second advisor for support and feedback whenever needed. Both always had an open ear for me and it was a pleasure to work with them.

Pierre Kirisci and Patrick Klein from BIBA supported my work with many discussions and concepts. I always enjoyed our work on projects.

I would like to thank the VICON team. Dr. Antoinette Fennell and Joshue O'Connor from CFIT, Dr. Yehya Mohamad and Svetlana Matiouk from Fraunhofer FIT, Haluk Gökmen from Arçelik, Thomas Bergdahl and Christina Johansson from DORO without whom the VICON project and so my thesis would not be successful.

Philipp Klaffert and Dr. Hannes Baumann supported me by comments and review of the final versions.

Finally, I would like to thank all other colleagues from the AI research group for numerous discussions on this thesis.

# Contents

# List of Figures

# List of Tables

# List of Theorems

# Abstract

In recent years more and more sophisticated devices are created including an, in the "worst" case, exponential growth of functionality: In current versions mobile phones are not just telecommunication devices, but also a camera, music player, browser, email interface etc., resulting in new terms like smart phones. A television device can also be used as a browser using a wireless internet connection and washing machines contain more programmable functions than customers will ever need and use. This complexity can most often be reflected as a burden for the users regarding the necessity to learn how to use such a product.

Accordingly, one main challenge - and opportunity - of human computer interaction is the involvement of each functionality in a respective and self-descriptive way to the user.

On the other hand, especially due to demographic changes, user requirements must also be considered in the design process. Existing guidelines and standards define approaches and recommendations regarding design issues related to different devices and user impairments, but are not consequently included in product development. Designers have the challenge to respect both topics and create either individual products or products for an as wide spread customer group of people as possible.

This thesis describes a possible approach, supporting designers with impact in product development phases from the first stage. While designers create product drafts and virtual prototypes, they are able to get concept information about end user needs and requirements before physical prototyping.

# Outline

This thesis consists of six chapters. The first chapter will present the background, motivation and all challenges within the topic of product development with focus upon elderly user groups. Also design recommendations are presented and clustered into semantic groups.

The second chapter has three main parts, relevant approaches of data representation, existing methods to infer data and similar solutions which deal with the topic of context awareness in product development.

The concept (chapter 3 and 4) represents an approach to the issue of inclusion regarding different end user scenarios focussing upon elderly and impaired beneficiaries, which was also used in the VICON[1] project.

Using the concept, an evaluation (chapter 5) was created with designers as test subjects. In Chapter 6 the result of the concept and additional future plans are discussed.

---

[1] See http://www.vicon-project.eu

# Chapter 1

# Introduction

## 1.1 Background and Motivation

The emergence of new embedded mobile technologies leads to a substantial growth of functionality in technical products. In turn, this growth in functionalities stimulates accessibility and economic issues. These issues contain accessibility and ergonomic issues regarding the use of product interfaces as the result of an overload of functions and capabilities.

For instance mobile phones are no longer just telecommunication devices, but also a camera, music player, browser, email interface etc., becoming smart phones. Devices with "voice calling capability, cellular connectivity and a screen size of at least 5, but less than 7 inches" are now called phablets (see Segan [2012]). Smaller and more efficient electronic components can be included into products, resulting in continuously expanding functionality. The fascination about new possibilities often obscures the fact that technology can also create new burdens and complexity to end users (see Woods [1996]). Especially a merge of different functionalities into single devices can be very inefficient regarding acceptance and usability by the end users.

This development can be seen as a two-edged sword, on the one side new functionality and features increase the product value, on the other side all new functionality and features must be included into a recognizable product, mostly resulting in a redefinition of the product. Also new interface components are often used to include more functionality on a small space. For instance operating the BMW iDrive interface (see figure 1.1) the user is able to control different tasks like navigation, radio or phone. The interface consists of a touch pad on the surface of a rotary switch which can be turned to specify a selection of the user or the user can draw on the touch

1

Figure 1.1: BMW iDrive controller and display (Source: BMW AG)

pad to perform more sophisticated tasks like browsing the internet.

Interfaces like the iDrive are capable realizing multiple functionalities, but the user needs to adapt and learn how to operate it properly (figure 1.1). This issue will most likely result in a lower acceptance by especially elderly people or people who often do not have the physical capabilities to interact with such as system. Human factors like the definition of motor capabilities are used to value these exact capabilities of end users.

This thesis focuses upon the support and application of inclusive design theories, principles and methods into the product development process to successfully integrate end user requirements, so the product can be used and accessed by the largest possible group of users (see Kirisci et al. [2011b] and Kirisci et al. [2011a]).
Different projects deal with this topic to change and maintain product development process by creating guidelines for designers to add background knowledge about the end users (further referred to as **beneficiaries**) of the products. One example is the exclusion calculator of the inclusive design toolkit (Clarkson [2003]), which defines what percentage of users of a target population can not perform a specific task (e.g. kneeling down). Other projects like TIRESIAS (Abbott [2007]) or CARDIAC (Cardiac Consortium [2012]) collect expertise based upon end-user studies, guidelines or other projects to present recommendations and information about design principles

and methods for different physical and non-physical products.

These guidelines can not immediately be integrated into the product development process, but rather should be seen as a type oriented textual collection of factors which should be advised while designing a product for beneficiaries. By the definition of beneficiaries of products, especially impaired and elderly people are addressed to maintain the ability to design a product as accessible and usable by an as wide range group of people as possible (see Newell and Gregor [2000]). This approach is also driven by the demographic change resulting from low birth rates and a higher life expectancy due to better medical treatment (see 1.2). Regarding the design process and from realization perspective, Personas based upon ethnographic user studies are used to describe beneficiaries (Goodwin [2002]).

Figure 1.2: Beneficiary user with mobile phone (Source: RNID [2010])

Figure 1.2 represents one main factor of inclusive design in general. The person in the picture holds a mobile phone and - derived from the facial expression of this person - she is not sure what to do or how to perform a specific task. This leads to the question of who is responsible for a proper interpretation of a product interface? The designer who should be aware of the user or the user who needs to learn how to operate the product interface properly.

With respect to the demographic change (see next section 1.2), this question becomes more important. With more elderly users of product interfaces, different user requirements must be considered while designing a product interface. Also different diseases of ageing, especially hearing, visual and manual dexterity impairments must be included in the product development process. For instance do users with low visual acuity have problems to find and press buttons if text fonts or push-buttons are too small.

Existing recommendations and design guidelines provide this kind of information about the needs and requirements of beneficiaries with respect to impairments of the users (see 1.3 and 1.4 for a detailed review). Sustainable interfaces must take as many issues as possible into account to maintain a proper use of a product, resulting in the question, which recommendations about different aspects for a specific product are important for which product and how they should be presented to designers to be accepted in the development of a product.

## 1.2 Targeted Impairments

Two challenges drive the idea of inclusive design: the demographic change and the growing number of functionalities, devices are able to perform.

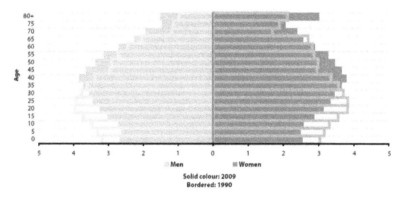

Figure 1.3: Population pyramid for EU-27 2009, excluding french overseas departments (Source: European Commission [2011])

Figure 1.3 (from European Commission [2011]) presents the population pyramid for 27 European countries for the years 1990 and 2009. Both life expectancy of women and men increased during this period. This demographic change to more elderly people does have an impact upon product customers, so user needs must be included in the product development process. Especially consumer products like mobile phones have a responsibility to act and adapt to these changes.

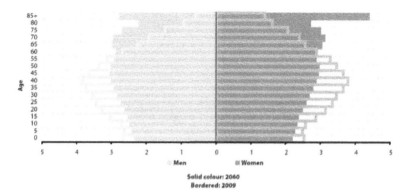

Figure 1.4: Projected population pyramid for EU-27 2060, excluding french overseas departments (Source: European Commission [2011])

Figure 1.4 (EUROPOP2008 convergence scenario, see European Commission [2011]) shows the projected population pyramid for the 27 European countries for the year 2060 compared to the pyramid of 2009. The amount of elderly people compared to 2009 will be much higher, resulting in a more extreme scenario.

In the VICON project, an ethnographic user study was carried out with elderly people (see 3.2). Out of this, various Personas were created defining average and abstract attributes for different mild to moderate impairments:

- Hearing Impairments
  Hearing impaired people have problems with acoustic feedback or acoustic involvement.

- Visual Impairments
  Visual impaired users have problems with too small visual output.

- Manual Dexterity Impairments
  Manual dexterity impaired users have grasp problem, e.g. if buttons are too small or too close together.

5

## 1.3  Inclusive Design

Design represents the process of creation. The concept of inclusive design deals with the capability to create and provide an interface, which can be theoretically used by everybody. This concept has gained many names (Design for All, Universal Design etc.). Newell and Gregor (Newell and Gregor [2000]) described inclusive design to be user sensitive with respect to the concept of universal usability. Langdon and Thimbleby directed the concept even more to demographic terms:

> *"The field of inclusive design relates the capabilities of the population to the design of products by better characterising the user–product relationship. Inclusion refers to the quantitative relationship between the demand made by design features and the capability ranges of users who may be excluded from use of the product because of those features."* (Langdon and Thimbleby [2010])

Various definitions of this concept are available, e.g. Clarkson et al. (Clarkson et al. [2003]), Persad et al. (Persad et al. [2007]), Keates et al. (Keates et al. [2000]) or Coleman and Lebbon (Coleman and Lebbon [2005]), but all refer to the same concept, to **adapt demographic changes of our society into the** product development process.

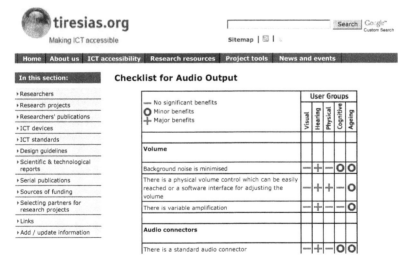

Figure 1.5: The TIRESIAS project website containing guidelines for designers (Source: Abbott [2007])

Currently the concept of inclusive design is referred to from many existing use studies and guidelines for designers. The TIRESIAS (Abbott [2007], see figure 1.5) and CARDIAC (Cardiac Consortium [2012], figure 1.6) projects collect these use studies into one website, presenting information which technical features, surfaces and issues must be adapted for different devices including mobile phones or remote controls.

These existing guidelines are not directly included in the design process of devices or in existing tools, used by designers with the consequence that most designers do not use them or even know about their existence.

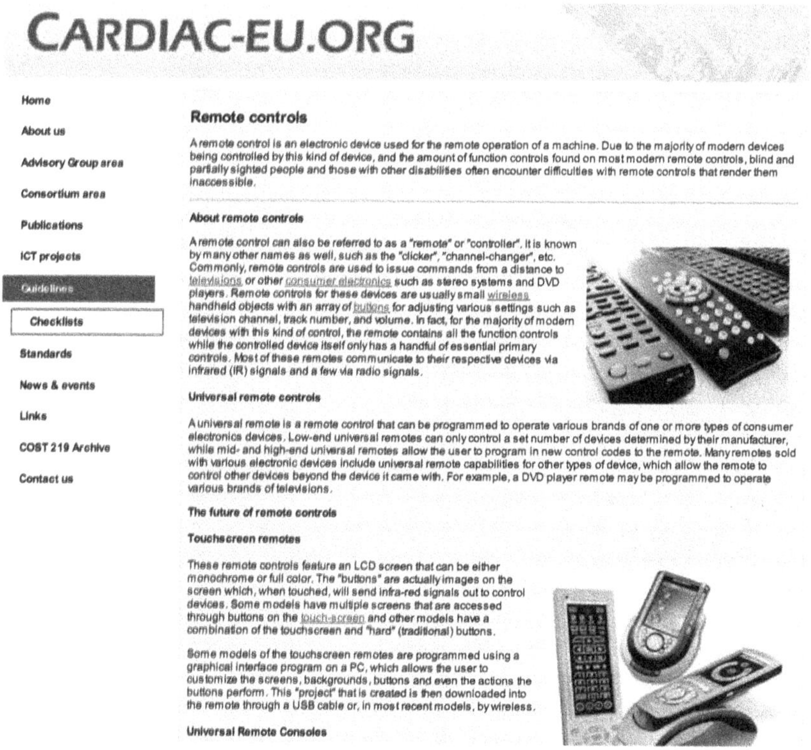

Figure 1.6: The CARDIAC project website containing guidelines for designers (Source: Cardiac Consortium [2012])

Regarding existing tools for designers, applications like the exclusion calculator of the inclusive design toolkit (Clarkson [2003]) focus upon a selective result of recommendations for designers based upon input of specific user impairments. Figure 1.7 presents the calculator and a selective input of requirements for visual, hearing, cognitive and manual dexterity impairments.

The output of the calculator is an exclusion value, which defines how much of the population is excluded by a specific design based upon a selection of different tasks within a product (see figure 1.8). For example, if the user input defines the task, which includes "bending down to reach various distances below the waist" to a level of kneeling down (demand level 3), the output of the tool presents an overall exclusion of 7.17% of the target population (gender: both, minimum age: 16, maximum age: 102).

Regardless, this output defines a task-related exclusion of a target population, there is no direct connection to any product capabilities except by the tasks. Furthermore no recommendations are presented, which should be considered if a product is designed, but rather tasks which should be avoided to include into a product.

Zitkus, Langdon and Clarkson (Zitkus et al. [2011]) compared various, already existing tools to support design teams to explore the accessibility value of a product (see chapter 2.5). Virtual techniques like DHM (Digital Human Modelling, see Duffy [2008]) support the development process during virtual product design phase, in which a target product is available in a virtual environment. A virtual human is able to perform different tasks including the product, but these tools mostly do not include impairments (see a more detailed review in chapter 2.5).

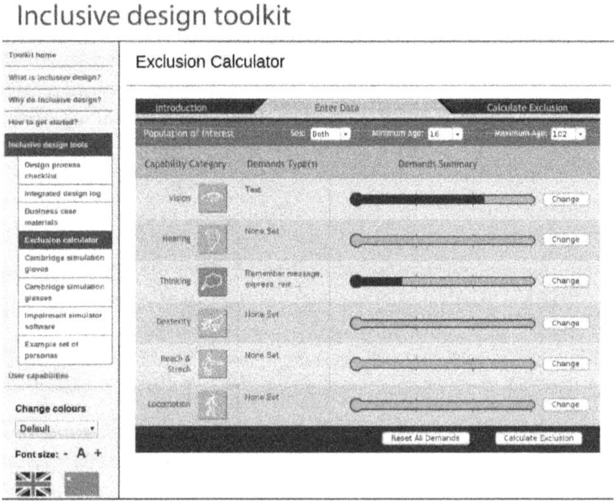

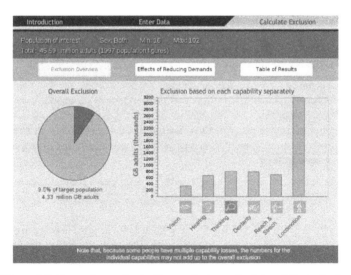

Figure 1.7: The exclusion calculator of the inclusive design toolkit (Source: Clarkson [2003])

Figure 1.8: Exemplary output of the exclusion calculator of the inclusive design toolkit (Source: Clarkson [2003])

## 1.4  Design Recommendations

Existing user studies and projects contain information about problems and issues regarding different kinds of user interfaces. These guidelines refer to a textual output of theories and data due to experience dealing with user needs of impaired customers of products. During the product development process designers need to have an as good awareness about user needs when dealing with problematic issues regarding the usage of each designed product as possible.

To maintain this awareness, the connection between the designers and beneficiaries of their products needs to be revised and optimised. Referring to the product development process a supporting system will be used to present and adapt issues of these guidelines and additional personal experience. The following example recommendation presents e.g. one issue derived from the TIRESIAS website.

> *"Visual markings on the keys should be characters at least 4 mm high and should have good contrast with the colour of the key (e.g. white characters on matt black keys)"* (see Abbott [2007])

This sentence defines already two very different recommendation with respect to requirements and user needs:

1. *Visual markings on the keys should be characters at least 4 mm high*
   This item defines an already specified minimum value for a font size of characters upon keys. Thus it refers to a nominal value, this issue type is defined as a **quantitative recommendation**.

2. *Good contrast with the colour of the key*
   With respect to nominal values, this issue refers to an abstract view on the product design interface. During the product development process it can be very problematic to adapt to these issues automatically due to all different assertions of natural speech. This type of information is referred to as **qualitative recommendations**.

Due to the differences between qualitative and quantitative recommendations, both types should be adapted and used separately.

Qualitative recommendations relate to non-measurable challenges of a design and can be very abstract (e.g. good contrast). Also relations and functional dependencies between values can be stated. For this qualitative recommendations need to be included in an early stage of the design process so designers are able to incorporate them.

Quantitative recommendations focus on nominal parameters of a design resulting in the need of an available (virtual) design of the product. These recommendations should be included in later design phases as parameters can change during the design of a product (e.g. total width of a device can be modified if a new button is added).

## 1.5 Research Questions

The focus of this thesis contains research questions extracted from all different fields of the inclusion of a supporting system into the product development process. First all different data must be usable included into a representation which can handle all different kind of data (textual information, images, further links etc.). This data must be used for a dynamic extraction to present only relevant data, which the designer needs based upon all input given as a selection of a specific impairment group of beneficiaries. The next issue is how to present the data to the user as seamless as possible in the product development process. Since designers use various (software or not software) tools e.g. draft sketches in a phase based sequence, all support must be included as much as possible in the typical design process.

Thus the following research questions are topic of this thesis:

- **Representation of information** - *How to extract data from issues?*
  One main requirement is to include both quantitative and qualitative recommendations into a database or context-aware system. (see section 1.4)

- **Adaptation of information** - *How to maintain adaptation and sustainability?*
  All recommendations must be manipulable including an addition of designer's personal experience.

- **Exploitation of information** - *How to use available data?*
  Each recommendation item must be represented in a designer-friendly way, the inclusion in different tools of the design process is preferred.

- **Impact without hindrance in the** product development process - *How to maintain designer acceptance?*
  All issues must be included in the product development process smoothly to maintain the acceptance by designers. This is a main point, which is also mentioned by various authors as problematic (see Clarkson et al. [2003], Dong et al. [2005], Goodman et al. [2006a], Goodman et al. [2006b], Dong et al. [2004] and Cassim and Dong [2007]).

## 1.6   Hypotheses

Based upon the research questions, the following hypotheses can be derived.

### Hypothesis 1 (*Ontology based model application*)

> *Ontology based models can be used to store and manipulate various data concerning requirements especially of elderly people for the use of products.*

This thesis also refers to the extraction and description of already available context information and requirements into one single knowledge management solution. It **must be possible, to include all kind of data** involved in the performance of a task by elderly. This will be addressed in chapter 3.

### Hypothesis 2 (*Suitable Reasoning*)

> *Ontology based models can be used to give statements from knowledge base for specified scenarios described by the questions of **who** is using a product **where** to perform **what** task.*

From the context information as presented in the first hypothesis, statements must be inferred so designers get only relevant information for specific scenarios. This refers to a general verification of all software-related terms (see chapter 4).

### Hypothesis 3 (*Designer acceptance*)

> *The involvement of context awareness for designers about impairments of product beneficiaries into different phases of product development provides adequate flexibility and designer acceptance by requirement traceability due to the focus of each phase upon different scenario issues.*

To obtain acceptance by designers, a high degree of usability is a mandatory factor for the implementation and realization of the system. If designers cannot adequately use the software included in their typical software environment, the approach would not support the user but rather hinder instead. The verification of this hypothesis can be separated into different issues which will be analysed and discussed in chapter 5.

## 1.7 Conclusion

This chapter introduced the need of to create a solution for supporting inclusive design during the product development process. With technological advances new functionality issues appeared regarding a balance between human capabilities and possible interactions when using a device. New devices were introduced (e.g. smart phones) which allow users to perform a higher amount of functionalities resulting in a higher complexity as seen in section 1.1. This complexity can most often be reflected as a burden for the users regarding the necessity to learn how to use such a product.

As seen in section 1.2, demographic changes must also be considered in the design process as there is an increasing number of elderly users of these devices. Inclusive design describes a concept how to deal the capabilities of beneficiaries to provide interfaces, which can be theoretically used by everybody. Guidelines and standards exist referring to approaches and recommendations presenting design issues with respect to devices and user impairments, but are not directly included in the product development process (section 1.3).

Section 1.4 presented the approach, how to separate these recommendations into quantitative and qualitative for later use. Research questions were defined to state the topic of this thesis (section 1.5) resulting in three hypotheses (section 1.6) regarding the possibility to use Ontology based models for storage of data, a suitable reasoning to describe scenarios and designer acceptance as designers are the end users of the framework.

Chapter 2 will present the relevant state of the art for the issue of supporting inclusive design during the product development process.

# Chapter 2

# State of the Art

An objective of this thesis is the storage and management of knowledge needed for the design process. The title of this thesis already raised one possible answer, defining Ontology-based models. The following section deals with the question of how and which kind of context-aware systems can be used for the representation, integration and inference of knowledge. This includes the manipulation of data and the creation of results based upon rules, relations and constraints.

## 2.1 Current Product Development Process

The product development process covers the product design from first creative ideas to the creation of the final prototype most often as a logical sequence of consecutive steps. The complete sequence of product development is most often separated into specific phases. The Association of German Engineers (VDI) described this process in various guidelines (see VDI-Gesellschaft Konstruktion und Entwicklung - Produktionstechnik (ADB) - Gemeinschaftsausschuß Produktplanung [1980], VDI-Gesellschaft Entwicklung Konstruktion Vertrieb [1993] and VDI-Gesellschaft Konstruktion und Entwicklung - Produktionstechnik (ADB) - Gemeinschaftsausschuß Produktplanung [2004]) which are established on an european level and often included into companies' structures (Vicon Consortium [2010a]). Especially VDI 2221 describes an accurate hierarchy based upon the main phases: draft phase, concept phase and elaboration phase ("Entwurfsphase", "Konzeptphase" and "Ausarbeitungsphase"), including a definition of requirements, functional parameters and drafts in the first, geometrical modelling and form design in the second and prototype construction in the third phase.

Since it is not possible to define a process, which is valid for all products and all issues[1], this thesis focuses upon a product development process including the first two phases, henceforth referred to as sketch design and CAD (computer-aided design) phases.

In the draft (sketch design) phase designers create prototype drafts. As already mentioned, the priority in this phase lies within the surface design, functional issues are not as relevant. Additionally these drafts are highly subjective, due to the influence by the designer's knowledge, creativity and preferences, which results in concentrated views on surface and form design that all functional aspects have to be adapted to.

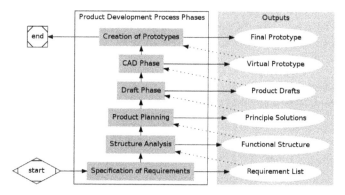

Figure 2.1: Product Development Process according to VDI-Gesellschaft Entwicklung Konstruktion Vertrieb [1993]

Concept design (or computer-aided design) phase describes the virtual construction of the previously designed drafts using computer-aided technologies (CAx) like Siemens NX. The product is specified including all parameters, values and surfaces resulting in a specification which is used for the construction of first (real) prototypes. With respect to the first phase, instead of a surface and form design, this

---

[1]Berthold described these and other methodologies and definitions for product development process (Berthold [2002]) and compared VDI guidelines with other definitions, resulting in the hypothesis:

"It is not possible to define a "right" construction methodology which is valid for all problems. The requirements are too different. On the one hand, different product groups result in different requirements for construction methodology, on the other hand engineering departments already have experience based upon the operational field of the company. Additionally, each designer has his own personal experiences and preferences which he prefers." (translation, for original text see Berthold [2002], p.35))

specification decomposes the product into parts and sub parts referring to functional requirements of the product. As a result, and based upon the form and surface of previous drafts, a concrete functional model can be seen in a virtual environment.

Figure 2.1 presents these phases in the product development process according to VDI-Gesellschaft Entwicklung Konstruktion Vertrieb [1993] (translation, see p.16 ff.). As already mentioned, in this thesis especially the phases "Draft Phase" and "CAD Phase" are focused upon by giving support for the creation of inclusive designed products.

## 2.2   Context Modelling

All aspects dealing with issues related to inclusive design must be representable. It is also necessary to ease the inclusion of facts and issues derived from guidelines and personal experience of designers into the database, to gain the advantage of manipulation of constraints directly.

The following example recommendation presents one type of user requirement, the system must be able to integrate into knowledge base.

> "Visual markings on the keys should be characters **at least 4 mm high** and should have **good contrast with the colour of the key** (e.g. white characters on matt black keys) (Gill [1997])."

This recommendation presents one example of what type of information needs to be included. Marked words define important contextual information, which needs to be transferred to a nominal or textual form into the knowledge base. It includes both qualitative and quantitative issues. The definition that the characters should be at least 4 mm high is a quantitative recommendation including a minimum value. On the contrary, the issue regarding the good contrast describes a qualitative recommendation, with an abstract definition.

Accordingly the following issues contain all main requirements for the system described in this thesis (see Strang and Linnhoff-Popien [2004] and Baldauf et al. [2007]).

1. **Comprehensible / human readable**
   To maintain a modification ability, the whole data structure should be human readable (e.g. XML). This would also ease the manipulation of the knowledge base.

2. **Dynamic Modifications**
   It must be possible to change and modify objects and structures of the data storage with respect to variability of knowledge.

3. **Models**
   A model based architecture is recommended (e.g. User Model, Task Model, Environment Model) to separate objectives for each knowledge part.

## 2.2.1 Key-Value Models

Key-Value models define the most simple data structure for context modelling (see Strang and Linnhoff-Popien [2004] and Baldauf et al. [2007]). The main idea is to add information as a pair of information, connecting one keyword with another word or nominal value. Formally, key-value models can be defined as a set of:

$$KV = (K_i, V_i)$$

The main advantage and disadvantage by using key value models is the unique binding of each key $K_i$ to exactly one value $V_i$. The models, derived from this structure, are also not able to describe relations and functions between keys directly, resulting that these models would not be suitable for a representative structure in case of describing issues and recommendations as mentioned above.

## 2.2.2 Markup Scheme Models

Markup Scheme models mainly concentrate upon the representation of hierarchies upon profiles. In this context especially three approaches are mentioned: Composite Capabilities / Preference Profile (CC/PP) (Kiss [2006]), Comprehensive Structured Context Profiles (CSCP, see Held et al. [2002]) and User Agent Profile (Forum [2001]). Each describes subjects (e.g. users, components) as profiles including categorical and nominal values as a Resource Description Language (RDF, see Lassila et al. [1998]) based meta language.

### 2.2.3 Graphical Models

Context can also be described as graphical profiles and relations e.g. using Unified Modeling Language (UML) Rumbaugh et al. [2004]. UML diagrams combine elements focusing upon the direct representation of relational data.

For instance Hendricksen et al. (Henricksen et al. [2005]) presented a context extension to the object-role modelling (ORM) approach by Haplin et al. (Halpin et al. [2008]) as presented in figure 2.2, in which different facts of context information is described as entities and facts(Strang and Linnhoff-Popien [2004]).

### 2.2.4 Object Oriented Models

Object oriented models like the cues, as presented by Schmidt and Van Laerhoven (Schmidt and Van Laerhoven [2001]), mainly focus upon encapsulation and fusion of data. Baldauf, Dustdar and Rosenberg (Baldauf et al. [2007]) described these models to offer "the full power of object orientation (e.g. encapsulation, re-usability, inheritance)". Accordingly these factors, to be able to divide all kind of information and build relations between them, is one main requirement for the topic of this thesis, object oriented models define a possible solution.

### 2.2.5 Logic Based Models

Logic based models offer a very high degree of formality (see Baldauf et al. [2007] and Strang and Linnhoff-Popien [2004]), including a possibility to use information to infer results based upon rules or relations. This reasoning step is able to add, update or delete context information automatically with the requirement of a strong formalisation.

### 2.2.6 Ontology Based Models

The term Ontology originally comes from the field of philosophy, meaning the study of existence. Ontology based models are used in various approaches like the VUMS cluster projects VERITAS (Chalkia et al. [2010]), VICON (Kirisci et al. [2011b], Kirisci et al. [2011a]), GUIDE (Hamisu et al. [2011]) and MyUI (Peissner et al. [2011]). Wang et al. presented an Ontology based context model, which is feasible and also includes reasoning schemas (Wang et al. [2004]).

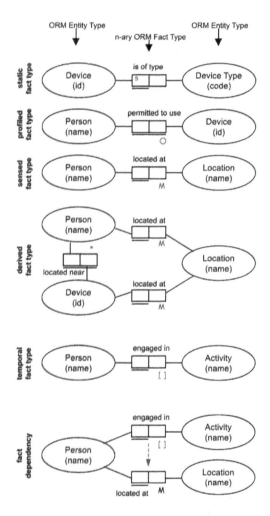

Figure 2.2: Contextual Extended ORM (Source: Strang and Linnhoff-Popien [2004])

19

Staab and Studer (Staab and Studer [2009]) presented a sophisticated definition about Ontology techniques and applications. Ontology in general can be formally described by:

$$O = (C, R, A^0)$$

where $C$ can be defined as the context, $R$ as relations and $A^0$ as axioms.

## 2.3 Expert Systems

One main topic of artificial intelligence (AI) addresses the question of how to define and solve problems. In terms of this work, section 2.2 describes possible approaches of a knowledge base. Furthermore section 2.3 deals with the question of how to use, connect and infer the data for a manipulable system as required. These systems are referred to as expert systems.

Requirements as presented in 1.5 as well as daily life situations are governed by deterministic rules. Rule-based expert systems represent an efficient and comprehensive way to handle knowledge base information by functions and inference. The concept of expert systems emerged in the late 1960s (see Davis et al. [1977]), including systems like DENDRAL (Lindsay et al. [1993]) or MYCIN (Shortliffe [1976]) which focus upon the medical field using rule based engines. Analogously Schank and Riesbeck (1981) wrote:

> "AI has gotten into the knowledge business in a big way in the late few years, partially because of the success of MYCIN, DENDRAL and other programs." (see Schank and Riesbeck [1981])

Since then the field of expert systems grew continuously, extended and was used in new domains (see Castillo and Alvarez [1991], Castillo et al. [1997], Hayes-Roth et al. [1984], Waterman [1986] and Giarratano and Riley [1998]). Otherwise, the field of ontologies is growing similarly as expert systems, (see Wache et al. [2001], Staab and Studer [2009] and Russell and Norvig [2010]) filling the gap between knowledge management and reasoning.

Current expert systems, implementing ontologies as a knowledge base, concentrate upon more domain specific approaches like KONWERK (see Günter and Hotz [1999] and Funke and Sebastian [1996]). KONWERK represents a modular configuration tool which is able to perform domain specific reasoning including the specification of a task (configuration aim), objects, relations and previous knowledge about the configurational process. Objects function as instances, which can inherit properties representing e.g. domain specific preferences. Using constraint-propagation, value ranges of the problem domain are successive narrowed by interpolation of constraints.

KONWERK consists of four basic modules focusing upon the following general tasks:

- Representation of domain objects:
  Domain objects define various models or virtual representations of all objects, which are or can be involved in the problem domain area.

- Representation and processing of relations, constraints and heuristics:
  Relations between all objects are used for the problem definition.

- Formulation of the configuration task:
  The task represents the problem that should be modelled. Objectives or criteria for the goal system, which should be maximized or minimized by selecting or constructing an appropriate solution, must be defined to process a suitable configuration.

- Control of the configuration task:
  In addition the configuration task must be manipulable by the user to change the goal if necessary.

The first step in developing a knowledge base of a specific domain consists of the definition of all different concepts involved in a problem. Figure 2.3 presents an example hierarchy, in which all objects are derived from the most general root object. Hence the taxonomy level of an object description defines, how specific a concept is. E.g. "Main River" is a "River" and "River" is an "Object".

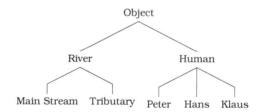

Figure 2.3: KONWERK - example hierarchy of concepts

All objects also can consist of different parameters like the length of a river or the name of a person. The following example from fig. 2.3 represents a constraint for the oxygen saturation of a river with minimum value.

```
1    (def-conceptual-constraint
2          :name        oxygensaturation_of_rivers
3          :patterns    ((?riv    :name river))
4          :formula     ("?riv.oxygenmin  <= 10")
```

Figure 2.4: KONWERK - example definition of a constraint

In the first line of figure 2.4, the name of the constraint is given. Lines 2-4 define various attributes of this constraint as a pair of keys and values. The formula is using the attribute of the river *oxygenmin* as a variable, representing if the variable of a river is less then 10 mg $O_2$/l. The river is included in the set of outputs.

In summary, expert systems like MYCIN represent a quite prominent approach of rule formalisms for knowledge representation in general. This is reflected in the dialect of the rules interchange format (RIF is still in development and only available as a draft version, see also Kifer [2011] and Kifer [2008]) of the W3C[1].

# 2.4 Customer involvement in product development

This chapter presents approaches for incorporation of human factors into the product development process. M. A. Kaulio (Kaulio [1998]) presented a review on selected methods of user involvement and compared seven different methods by the categories of customer involvement: *design for*, *design with* and *design by*. *Design for* denotes approaches in which products are designed without a direct confrontation with customers. Products are created by designers using data, general theories and models of customer behaviour instead. *Design with* focuses on a similar product design process as *design for* approaches but including a presentation of concepts and prototypes to customers. Feedback is used in product design for adaptations of products to end user needs. In the last category of *design by*, customers are actively involved in product development and create products. Using these categories, the following customer involvement methods were compared:

- Quality function deployment (QFD)
  Quality function deployment was introduced by Yoji Akao in 1983 (see Akao [2004]) and describes an analytical approach for the first design phases with the involvement of end users. It represents the conversion of consumer demands into quality characteristics and the iterative development of a design quality function describing a "relation" between consumer and product. In QFD, the

---

[1]http://www.w3.org/2005/rules/wiki/RIF_Working_Group

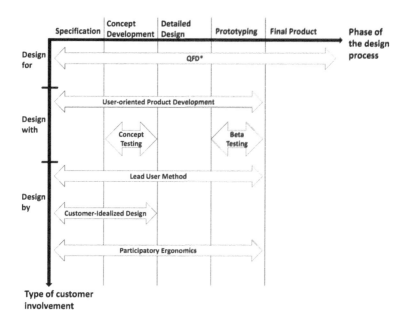

Figure 2.5: Methods of involvement reviewed (**Source:** Kaulio [1998])

only contact point of designers and consumers is before the creation of the product to specify all relevant parameters.

- User-oriented product development
  In relation to QFD, user-oriented product development focuses upon the involvement of the user after the first prototype creation. It includes an use-analysis phase into product development, in which prototypes of the target product are used by beneficiaries (Rosenblad-Wallin [1985]). Due to cost intensive prototype generation, this method is mostly suitable for products, in which functional issues are primarily important.

- Concept testing
  This method connects first sketch designs of the target product with an evaluation by customers. Concept testing should be supplemented with later prototype evaluations, e.g. beta testing (Moore [1982]).

- Beta testing
  Using a prototype of the target product, beta testing refers to a field test with customers. Due to the fact that a prototype must already be available, this

method should also not be the only method for feedback by end users and supplemented by methods applied to earlier phases. It is most frequently used in software engineering (Fine [2002]).

- Consumer idealized design
  Consumer idealized design involves end users into product development immediately (Ciccantelli and Magidson [1993]). In this approach customers create a design with support by a facilitator in a group exercise. Participants select first representatives of the target market, or several representatives for several target groups of the product. The representatives create: A (new) design, a list of articulated requirements and a record of underlying reasons for the design choices.

- Lead user method
  In this approach, "lead users" represent users who face needs that will be general in a marketplace - but face them months or years before the bulk and expect to benefit significantly by obtaining a solution to those needs (see Herstatt and Von Hippel [1992]). Due to the fact, that these users also find solutions with respect to their own needs, a more active involvement is possible.

- Participatory ergonomics
  Participatory ergonomics involves workers / users themselves actively as designers in the whole product development process (Haines et al. [1998]). By being a part of design and physical construction of the product, this approach focus upon experience of all participants of product development (Sundin et al. [2004]).

Figure 2.5 presents the outcome of the review of the above mentioned methods. In relation to different product development phases, each method has its pros and cons:

- Three main impact fields for customer involvement were identified. These include: specification, concept development and prototyping. Related to this thesis, a separation of product development into phases is suitable.

- There is no single best method for all products. The most suitable customer involvement method is defined by cost, time and suitability of end product.

- Customer involvement methods are used to get feedback and reactions stepwise or during product development. It is advantageous to create a possibility to include as much of this information into early stages of product development as possible.

As mentioned in the last point, a knowledge base including as much context information about end users is advantageous. In the next chapter 3 the possibility to create
a suitable knowledge base will be discussed.

## 2.5 Digital Human Models

In current design approaches, DHMs (digital human modelling) is used for a virtual
representation of humans in a virtual environment. DHMs like RAMSIS or JACK (and
his female counterpart JILL) are already well accepted by design teams in the product
development industry. They are able to perform different tasks using an avatar,
based upon anthropometric data sets (see also Naumann and Roetting [2007]).

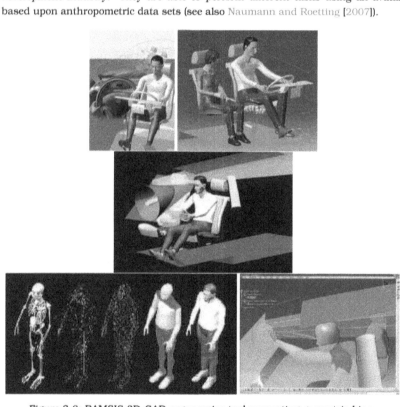

Figure 2.6: RAMSIS 3D-CAD-ergonomics tool presenting geometric kinematic digital human model (Source: Human Solutions GmbH
[2012])

Computer-based human models are currently widely used in the development of vehicle interiors, aircraft cockpits, passenger spaces and workplaces. The functions differ from the ergonomic design of driver and passenger areas to the overall design for an efficient maintenance and repair work.

An avatar (mannequin) is used for the representation of the beneficiary in both systems (see figure 2.6 for RAMSIS, figure 2.7 for JACK) . In the first step the designer creates a virtual environment, selects the avatar specifications and defines tasks. Using probabilistic posture prediction for the avatar performing these tasks, analysis output can present values for reachability, comfort or viewport.

Poirson and Delangle compared several DHM tools including RAMSIS, JACK, Sammie CAD, Anybody or MakeHuman (see Poirson and Delangle [2013]) through a list of 25 comparison criteria. Most DHMs do not include capabilities of users with impairments (see Zhou et al. [2009]) but rather anthropometric standards. Kaklanis et al. (Kaklanis et al. [2012b], see chapter 2.6.3 for a more detailed review) presented a different view including Virtual User Models for specification of impairment issues.

From the perspective of including user needs, DHM systems highly focus upon substantial design studies during product development process and are not able to give the designer recommendations, of how which parts of the product should be changed. Designers are able to perform tasks in a virtual environment and to identify e.g. reachability issues.

The presented tools focus on the evaluation of products in a virtual environment. As an input, a virtual prototype of the product must already be available. DHM tools are able to simulate tasks performed by virtual avatars providing indicators for ergonomic issues. In terms of this thesis, support of inclusive design must occur in earlier stages during first product drafts and CAD design.

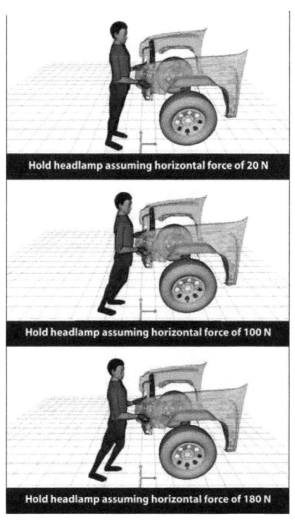

Figure 2.7: Digital Human Model JACK presenting the task "Hold Head-
lamp" with three different force magnitudes (Source: Zhou
et al. [2009])

## 2.6 Related Projects

This thesis was created within the context of the VICON project to support designers of physical products like mobile phones, washing machines or TV remotes by providing recommendations to include end user needs. VICON is a part of the VUMS cluster[1]. VUMS is a cluster that includes the projects VICON, GUIDE, MyUI and VERITAS. All projects work on improving the accessibility of several products and application areas, taking into account different impairments.

### 2.6.1 MyUI Project

The MyUI Project ("Mainstreaming Accessibility through Synergistic User Modelling and Adaptability") aims to create adaptive software user interfaces based on multi-

---

[1]See http://www.veritas-project.eu/vums/

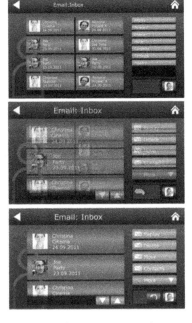

(1) **Before adaptation**: Permanent access to user profile and user interface profile via adaptation area (bottom right).

(2) **During adaptation**: Pulsing icon (here chameleon) indicates on-going adaptation.

(3) **After adaptation**: The user can undo the adaptation via button with curved backwards arrow.

Figure 2.8: Automatic adaptation with implicit confirmation (Source: Peissner et al. [2012])

modal design patterns (Peissner et al. [2012]).

A framework was implemented divided into 3 stages:

1. UI Parametrization:
   In the first stage parameters and variables valid for the output UI are defined. Variables include e.g. the font size, parameters e.g. the need for voice input. The data used in this stage is derived from the following sources:

   - Information about available input and output devices from the *Device Profile*
   - Information about user and environment from the *User Profile*
   - Customization settings that must be predefined by UI developers of applications from the *Customization Profile*

2. UI Preparation:
   Additionally the most suitable selection of UI components is made in this stage including the following input:

   - All possible application interactions are predefined in the *Abstract Application Interaction Model* which defines different situations for each state of the application.
   - To maintain the accessibility of the user interface, requirements for end users of the interface are specified in the *User Interface Profile* and are related to the current user, environment and device setup.

   After this preparation a complete set of information about the current user, device and interactions is available.

3. UI Generation and Adaptation:
   Based on previous data the interface is generated to user needs and can dynamic and system-initiated be UI adapted at runtime: If the user changes, the three stages of adaptation must be repeated.

   - User Interface Generation:
     This activity creates and renders the UI based on all provided data. The result is shown in the last image of figure 2.8 (see Peissner et al. [2012]).
   - User interface adaptations during use:
     The possibility to adapt the UI to the user is included. If for instance new components and elements have been selected, this activity triggers adaptations to the current available UI so the new components can be included at runtime.
   - Profile Updates:
     Regarding a user change, the stages must be re-initiated again triggered by this activity.

## 2.6.2   GUIDE Project

The GUIDE Project ("Gentle user interfaces for elderly people", see Langdon and Biswas [2012], Biswas et al. [2012] and Langdon [2013]) is targeting Web applications and related platforms. The aim is to create a software framework and design tools for developers to integrate accessibility issues and personalization features into applications.

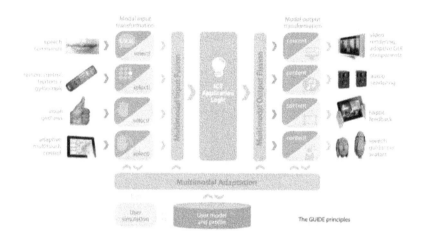

Figure 2.9: GUIDE - an open architecture for various multi-modal user interface technologies (Source: Jung and Hahn [2011])

By using a variety of human interaction modalities as e.g. speech commands or visual gestures, a logic controller can react and infer the most suitable configuration of an input device related to the customer (see figure 2.9). User Models including parameters describe end user capabilities regarding impairments, preferences are used by reasoning for scenario definition. These User Models are based on various tests and user trials with elderly and impaired customers (Jung and Hahn [2011]).

31

## Modelling Framework

For purpose of simulation and adaptation the GUIDE Project conducted different user trials. Three impairment levels for each modality of visual, hearing, manual dexterity and cognitive impairments were implemented based on a qualitative user study. The steps for this approach were (see Guide Consortium [2011]):

1. Obtain and collate survey data and user trial data

2. Reduce the dimensionality of the data set by eliminating highly correlated variables

3. Cluster the survey data for each modality: Vision, Hearing, Cognition, Physical

4. Reduce the dimensionality of the data set by eliminating non-significant variables in the k-means clustering

5. Take the resulting clusterings and characterize the cluster centres in terms of the combined contributions to the clusters.

6. Repeat for User trial data

7. Examine distance of users from cluster centres as indication of sensitivity to adaptation

8. Improve and refine with additional data and overlapping clustering techniques.

The full data set contains 46 users with different impairments at the age range of 49-90 years. It includes a variety of parameters to specific capabilities of each user.

Based on these parameters a k-means Clustering was applied with 3 clusters for low, medium and high levels for each impairment type (k=3, see Kanungo et al. [2002]). Non-significant variables were eliminated due to their contribution to the final clustering. The following tables 2.1 and 2.2 presents the resulting classification into each level without non-significant variables.

| Vision | | | |
|---|---|---|---|
| Close vision: level able to read perfectly | 20/20 | 20/60 | 20/80 |
| Distant vision: level able to read perfectly (metres) | 5 | 5 | 20 |
| General eyesight | good | excellent | normal |
| Seeing at distance | good | poor | poor |
| Seeing at night | normal | poor | poor |
| Colour perception | good | bad | bad |
| **Hearing** | | | |
| Able to hear a sound of 500Hz? | Yes | Yes | No |
| Able to hear a sound of 1Khz? | Yes | Yes | Yes |
| Able to hear a sound of 2Khz? | Yes | Yes | Yes |
| Able to hear a sound of 3Khz? | Yes | Yes | Yes |
| Able to hear a sound of 4Khz? | Yes | Yes | No |
| Able to hear a sound of 8Khz? | Yes | No | No |
| How do you define your hearing? | excellent | good | poor |
| Conversation from a noisy background | excellent | normal | normal |
| Movie dialogue only | excellent | good | poor |
| Ringing noises only | excellent | good | normal |
| Phone rings with a movie in background | excellent | good | poor |
| **Manual Dexterity** | | | |
| Mobility diagnosis | none | hernia / slipped disc | none |
| Muscular weakness | never | A few occasions | Frequently |
| Write | No difficulty | No difficulty | Mild difficulty |
| Push a heavy door | No difficulty | No difficulty | Mild difficulty |
| Change a bulb | No difficulty | No difficulty | Mild difficulty |
| Use of transport (bus, etc.) | No difficulty | No difficulty | Moderately difficult |
| Tingling of limb | No difficulty | Mild difficulty | Mild difficulty |
| Weakness | No difficulty | Mild difficulty | Moderately difficult |
| Rigidity | No difficulty | Mild difficulty | Moderately difficult |

Table 2.1: GUIDE Manual Dexterity related k-means Cluster Centres as a result of user survey (Source: Guide Consortium [2011])

| Cognition | | | |
|---|---|---|---|
| TMT[1] (seconds) | 30 | 49 | 136 |
| AVLT[2] series 1 (Short Term Memory: trial 1) | 10/15 words | 7/15 words | 5/15 words |
| AVLT series 2 (Short Term Memory: trial 2) | 11/15 words | 9/15 words | 6/15 words |
| AVLT series 3(Short Term Memory: trial 3) | 13/15 words | 9/15 words | 6/15 words |
| AVLT series 4 (Short Term Memory: trial 4) | 14/15 words | 10/15 words | 7/15 words |
| AVLT series 5 (Short Term Memory: trial 5) | 7/15 words | 5/15 words | 3/15 words |
| WAIS[3] - digit-symbol test (symbols written in 2 minutes) | 75 | 30 | 20 |

Table 2.2: GUIDE Cognition related k-means Cluster Centres as a result
of user survey (Source: Guide Consortium [2011])

Regarding cognitive tests, different learning tests were executed. During the AVLT (Auditory verbal learning test) 15 words had to be learned during 5 different trials. After each trial, participants were asked to recall as many words as possible. In the WAIS digital symbol test of table 2.2 participants were asked to combine single characters from different rows with each other. Each number from one row belongs to a character in the second row. The final score presented in the table is the amount of character-combinations written in 2 minutes.

**Simulation Platform**

The parameters were used to create a User Model for simulation of impairments. During the User Initialisation Application customers generate their specific User Model which is classified by the definition of the k-means cluster as seen in the previous section.

Figure 2.10 shows the web interface of the GUIDE Project for user initialisation. Different aspects of customer needs and preferences are defined based on selection and behaviour including visual, hearing, manual dexterity and cognitive capabilities of the end user. The resulting User Model can be used as a specification for the definition of an optimized accessible user interface. For instance a suitable color

---

[1]Trail Making Test, see Reitan [1986]
[2]Auditory verbal learning test, see Ivnik et al. [1990]
[3]Wechsler Adult Intelligence Scale, see Wechsler [1955]

configuration of buttons of a TV application are defined by the selection of the user as seen in figure 2.10.

The User Model can be used by customers to personalize their own device, but also as a simulation for application developers. Figure 2.11 presents such a simulation including a Social TV application without and with mild visual impairments.

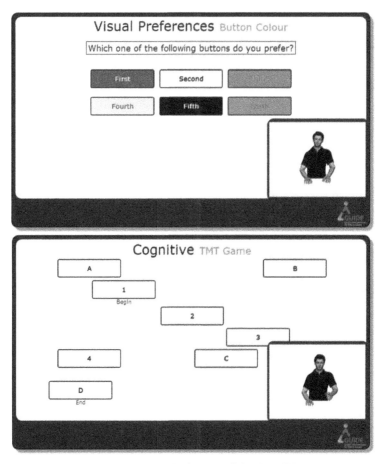

Figure 2.10: User Initialisation Application of the GUIDE Project (Source: GUIDE Consortium [a])

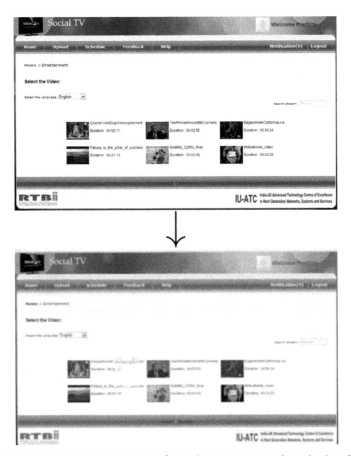

Figure 2.11: GUIDE Simulation of visual impairments without (top) and
with mild visual impairment (bottom) (Source: GUIDE Consortium [b])

36

## 2.6.3 VERITAS Project

The VERITAS Project ("Virtual and Augmented Environments and Realistic User Interactions To achieve Embedded Accessibility Designs") focuses on a virtual simulation framework including end user impairments to infer problematic usability issues (Kaklanis et al. [2012b]). Using this, designers are able to simulate end user behaviour when performing predefined tasks with virtual product prototypes. Contextual models including various general values but also impairment specific values were implemented to generate a realistic virtual scenario (Kaklanis et al. [2010]). A database of target users including nominal and categorical values for impairments and characteristics of elderly users was created to maintain a precise simulation (Moschonas et al. [2012]).

Table 2.3 exemplifies values for different impairment profiles which are included in the Virtual User Model. These values are used for different measurements in virtual environments to create results as presented in table 2.4. The table displays different attributes related to the virtual humanoid which are included in the User Model (physical characteristics). Normal values represent nominal range values, if the virtual humanoid represents a user that does not have any impairment. The other values define degrees of freedom for rheumatoid arthritis (Peña-Guevara et al. [2005]), spinal cord injury (Eriks-Hoogland et al. [2009]), adhesive shoulder capsulitis (Kazemi [2000]), hemiparesis (Zackowski et al. [2004]) or an average elderly man between 75 and 79 years. For instance a User Model with rheumatoid arthritis has a major impairment in the ranges for shoulder flexion, shoulder abduction and shoulder external rotation.

### Modelling Framework

The modelling framework in VERITAS consists of 3 different parts. All parts consist of context information that are necessary for the Simulation Platform. UsiXML was used to implement preferences and attributes (see Limbourg et al. [2005]).

1. Virtual User Model
   Similar as in this thesis, Virtual User Models were used to describe user needs and requirements. However, the model includes general preferences, disabilities, affected tasks, motor, visual, hearing, speech and cognitive and behavioural parameters.

2. Task Model
   The interaction between the virtual user and the environment is described in the

| Physical character-istics | Normal values | Rheuma-toid arthritis | Spinal cord injury | Adhesive shoulder capsulitis | Hemi-paresis | Elderly Man 75-79 |
|---|---|---|---|---|---|---|
| Wrist flexion | 0-60° | | | | | 0-62° |
| Wrist extension | 0-60° | | | | 0-67.48° | 0-53° |
| Shoulder flexion | 0-180° | 0-10° | 0-118° | 0-20° | 0-53.39° | |
| Shoulder abduction | 0-90° | 0-15° | 0-74° | 0-10° | | |
| Shoulder internal rotation | 0-90° | | | | | |
| Shoulder external rotation | 0-50° | 0-15° | 0-31° | 0-10° | | |
| Forearm supination | 0-85° | | | | | |
| Elbow flexion | 0-150° | | | 0-91.09° | | |

Table 2.3: Part of Virtual User Models as used in the VERITAS project (Source: Kaklanis et al. [2010])

Task Model. Complex tasks are divided into primitive tasks and must be pre-defined by designers / developers according to the functionality of the designed prototype.

3. Simulation Model

   The aim of the Simulation Model is to define all specific functionalities of the simulation result including information about possible tasks that can be performed during simulation by the virtual user.

**Simulation Platform**

To the VERITAS Simulation input is a Virtual User Model, a Simulation Model, one or more Task Models and a virtual 3D environment as part of the Simulation Platform. The Simulation Module creates a complete scenario in which the User Model performs tasks. The Simulation Platform has three elements:

1. Task Manager Module

   All task related issues are included in the Task Manager Module. It divides the selected task into primitive tasks and manages the humanoid to perform each task separately.

2. Humanoid Module

The skeletal model of any selected user consists of 46 elements and 45 joints, including different geometrical but also kinematic data, as degrees of freedom.

3. Scene Module

This module creates the complete scene including objects and their attributes.

| | Task | Rheumatoid arthritis | Spinal cord injury | Adhesive shoulder capsulitis | Hemiparesis | Elderly |
|---|---|---|---|---|---|---|
| Drawers on desk | Open top drawer | Simulation result: Failure – Shoulder joint limit *(a1)* | Simulation result: Success *(b1)* | Simulation result: Failure – Shoulder joint limit *(c1)* | Simulation result: Success *(d1)* | Simulation result: Success *(e1)* |
| | Open bottom drawer | Simulation result: Failure – Shoulder joint limit *(a2)* | Simulation result: Success *(b2)* | Simulation result: Failure – Shoulder & Wrist joint limit *(c2)* | Simulation result: Success *(d2)* | Simulation result: Success *(e2)* |
| Drawers below desk | Open top drawer | Simulation result: Failure – Shoulder joint limit *(a3)* | Simulation result: Success *(b3)* | Simulation result: Failure – Shoulder joint limit *(c3)* | Simulation result: Success *(d3)* | Simulation result: Success *(e3)* |
| | Open bottom drawer | Simulation result: Failure – Shoulder & Elbow & Wrist joint limit *(a4)* | Simulation result: Failure – Wrist joint limit *(b4)* | Simulation result: Failure – Shoulder & Elbow joint limit *(c4)* | Simulation result: Success *(d4)* | Simulation result: Success *(e4)* |

Table 2.4: Simulation results of the VERITAS project (Source: Kaklanis et al. [2010])

39

An exemplary output of the VERITAS Project framework is presented in table 2.4. Each task is performed by a virtual humanoid with different impairments like rheumatoid arthritis resulting in a value for success or failure and the problem issue.

### 2.6.4 VICON

As previously mentioned this thesis evolved during the VICON project providing there a supporting framework for designers during product development process. VICON aims to provide support to designers during the complete product development life cycle, allowing designers a recommendation-driven product development as presented by this thesis, but also to evaluate virtual products in a predefined virtual environment. The virtual simulation platform VIRTEX is used to create a comprehensive scenario and to test single tasks using an avatar of the beneficiary and the product (see Matiouk et al. [2013]). Figure 2.12 presents the simulation input of VIRTEX, including the import of a VSF file, which is used to store all input data from the first 2 phases (left, see also section 4.1.4) and the selection of User Profile and Environment (right picture).

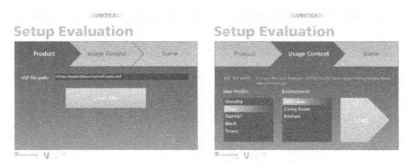

Figure 2.12: Simulation input of VIRTEX (Source: Vicon Consortium [2012b])

The VICON project product development life cycle consists of 3 phases: Sketch design phase, CAD phase and Evaluation phase. During sketch design phase designers are using the software tool of this thesis (see chapter 4.2.1) to create first product drafts. In CAD phase the integrated module in the CAD software Siemens NX is used (see 4.2.3) to get recommendations during the creation of a virtual prototype of the product. The third phase deals with additional tests and simulations including impairments of beneficiaries. In the first step of the evaluation, designers need to select a user profile with an already included predefined virtual humanoid and the

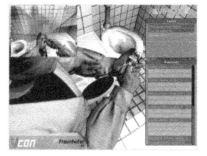

Figure 2.13: Simulation interface of VIRTEX (Source: Vicon Consortium [2012b])

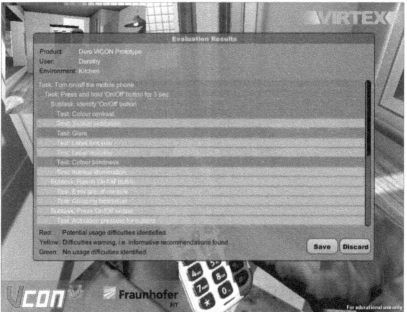

Figure 2.14: Simulation output of VIRTEX (Source: Vicon Consortium [2012b])

virtual environment in which the product should be used. The simulation performs a predefined set of tasks related to a specific device type. During the simulation (see figure 2.13) the virtual humanoid performs each subtask resulting in a classification if the task was successful or a failure, marked with a green and red background for each task. Currently processed tasks are marked yellow.

The output of the system also includes recommendations that are related to each task. Figure 2.14 presents such an output testing a mobile phone prototype.

### 2.6.5 Comparison

| MyUI | Creation of software adaptive user interfaces with respect to end user impairments |
|---|---|
| GUIDE | Creation of a software framework for designers to create adaptive TV interfaces for elderly people |
| VERITAS | Support designers in product development by a complex simulation framework including end user impairments |
| VICON | Support designers by giving recommendations in early phases and virtual simulation for evaluation of virtual prototype. |

Table 2.5: Focus of related projects

Table 2.5 presents the focus of each project like software development for different scenarios (MyUI, GUIDE) as well as physical user interface development (VERITAS, VICON) including aspects of impaired end users to create more customer-oriented products. In each project user trials were conducted and a XML/Ontology approach was driven to reflect scenarios.

## 2.7 Conclusion

In this chapter the current state of the art with respect to the topic as presented in chapter 1 was defined. In the first section 2.1, product development process from a general point of view was elaborated, resulting in the specification of phases in which design support is possible and needed. The phases "Draft Phase " and "CAD Phase" were identified as suitable for a quantitative and qualitative support during product development process. In section 2.2 several context modelling approaches were presented including concise definitions of each method. Based upon the investigations conducted in chapter 2, chapter 3 will present a survey in which each method will be compared using a selection of requirements.

Next to context modelling approaches, expert systems were introduced as an alternative approach, in which the user is able to configure concepts as a representation of a specified scenario as seen in section 2.3.

In section 2.4 seven customer involvement methods were reviewed resulting in the need of Virtual User Model to include as much information about beneficiaries as possible. This section describes the motivation for the next chapter.

DHMs were described in 2.5 as virtual product prototype evaluation tools, which allow designers to simulate tasks performed by virtual avatars indicating ergonomic issues, but for the simulation a virtual prototype must already be available. With respect to results of the first and fourth section of this chapter (see section 2.1 and 2.4), a support at an early stage is advantageous and will be further focused.

Related projects of this field with similar approaches were analysed in section 2.6 with different purposes. The projects MyUI and GUIDE focus on software development issues regarding requirements of elderly people while VERITAS and VICON relate to a supporting framework for designers. All projects conducted user trials for a scenario definition by an XML/Ontology approach. The next chapter will present the knowledge management approach used in this thesis.

# Chapter 3

# Knowledge Management

## 3.1 Context Modelling

With respect to the state of the art of context-aware systems, Strang and Linnhoff-Popien (Strang and Linnhoff-Popien [2004]) presented a survey based upon demands on context modelling approaches. The conclusion of the survey indicates that Ontology based models fulfil most of the requirements to ubiquitous computing systems. Regarding requirements of the creation of a knowledge base including human, environment, task and other factors in terms of this thesis, a different main focus is aimed:

1. Partial validation (*pv*)
   Due to requirements of this thesis, various models and relationships must be described, e.g. User Model profiles or recommendations based upon different values. Additionally a correct syntactical inference is needed for the purpose to provide accurate data and correct scenarios.

2. Level of formality (*for*)
   The level of formality describes how precise contextual facts and interrelationships between instances and models can be represented. Regarding requirements as presented in this thesis, formality is a very important issue to indicate different values (abstract, nominal etc.) in one and the same model.

3. Applicability to existing environments (*app*)
   Applicability represents the possibility to use the knowledge base in different other applications. This feature is relevant especially regarding future possibilities like import of and export into other knowledge bases.

4. Distributed composition (dc)
   This requirement is irrelevant with respect to existing server-client architecture

for maintenance purposes (see requirement dossier of the VICON project (Vicon Consortium [2011a]))

5. Richness and quality of information (qua)

   With respect to sensorial data, this requirement describes support for quality and richness of incoming data. This issue is not relevant in cases of this thesis.

6. Incompleteness and ambiguity (inc)

   This issue represents the importance of the feature to manipulate and use data, even if it is incomplete. Regarding the VICON project, this issue is not important, due to the non existence of sensorial data.

| Approach | pv | for | app | dc | qua | inc |
|----------|----|----|----|----|----|----|
| Key-Value Models | - | - | + | - | - | - |
| Markup Scheme Models | ++ | + | ++ | + | - | - |
| Graphical Models | - | + | + | - | + | - |
| Object Oriented Models | + | + | + | ++ | + | + |
| Logic Based Models | - | ++ | - | ++ | - | - |
| Ontology Based Models | ++ | ++ | + | ++ | + | + |

Table 3.1: Results according to Strang and Linnhoff-Popien (Source: Strang and Linnhoff-Popien [2004])

With respect to thesis related requirements, *pv*, *for* and *app* requirements are primarily important[1]. Table 3.1 (see Strang and Linnhoff-Popien [2004]) presents a comparison between all different approaches including an appropriateness value for each of them. In consequence, Ontology based models are most suitable for the implementation of a knowledge base.

Regardung the theses presented in 1.6, Ontology based models would be suitable for the implementation of all requirements for elderly people. In the next chapter and using Ontology based models, a separation between initial (3.3) and inferred Ontology(3.4.4) will be presented, including a reasoning step including an application of specific rule sets to the initial model (3.4).

---

[1]++ means a complete, + a partial and − no fulfilment of the requirement.

## 3.2  User Study

With respect to the topic of the VICON project[1], a detailed ethnographic research was carried out with involvement of a group of elderly people and designer groups. This user study was executed by Royal National Institute for Deaf People (RNID) 2010 (see Vicon Consortium [2010]) and involved a test scenario including washing machines and mobile phones.

The target group contained 58 elderly people who had a range of three different types of mild-to-moderate WHO classified impairments (see Stucki [2005]): Hearing loss (B230), sight loss (B210) and manual dexterity (B710/730). Each participant had either one minor developed physical impairment or a combination of all target impairments.

Figure 3.1 presents the age groups of all 58 participants. With respect to their impairments, the age is relevant in order to ensure the classification of mild-to-moderate impairments.

---

[1]The aim of this thesis refers to a part of the VICON project (**Vi**rtual User **Con**cept for Supporting Inclusive Design of Consumer Products and User Interfaces). The project deals with the support through the complete product development phases including an evaluation of the target product in a virtual environment.

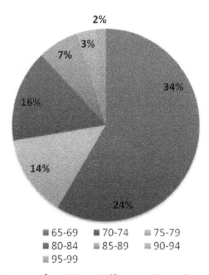

Figure 3.1: Age groups of participants (Source: Vicon Consortium [2010])

### 3.2.1 Impairments

Before execution of a user study the first question relates to impairments and their definition. Hearing impairment represent a total or partial loss of hearing ability in one or both ears (ICF B230, see Organization et al. [2012a]). With respect to this study, a classification based upon the European Group on genetics of hearing impairments (EGGHI) was used (see Martini [1996] and table 3.2[1]). Similar definitions can be found from the British Society of Audiologistics (BSA) and the Royal National Institute for Deaf and Hard of Hearing People (RNID), consequently indicating, that there is a consensus for four hearing impaired levels (see Vicon Consortium [2010] and table 3.2).

Vision can be described as sensory function relating to sensing the presence of light and sensing the form, size, shape and colour of the visual stimuli (B210, see Organization et al. [2012b]).

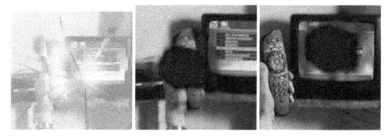

Figure 3.2: Simulation of a vision impairment with cataracts (left) and macular degeneration (middle and right) (Source: Vicon Consortium [2010])

A wide range of tests exists to measure different types of vision or vision impairments. Vision impairments can be very different, due to specific issues dealing with sensorial functionality (see examples in Vicon Consortium [2010]). The most familiar method of tests is the assessment of visual acuity using the Snellen chart (see Snellen [1863]) where a series of individual letters, decreasing in size, are presented on a wall chart and the person is asked to read the chart from a specified distance.

The resulting measure of visual acuity (VA) indicates an individual's ability to read the chart in comparison with an individual with perfect visual acuity. Determined

---

[1]Audiometric Descriptors are based on the average of the pure tone hearing threshold levels at 250, 500, 1000, 2000 and 4000Hz

| Audiometric descriptors | Definitions of hearing loss (dB) |
|---|---|
| Mild hearing loss | On average, the most quiet sounds that people can hear with their better ear are **between 25 and 40 dB**. People who suffer from mild hearing loss have some difficulties keeping up with conversations, especially in noisy surroundings. |
| Moderate hearing loss | On average, the most quiet sounds heard by people with their better ear are **between 40 and 70 dB**. People who suffer from moderate hearing loss have difficulty keeping up with conversations when not using a hearing aid. |
| Severe hearing loss | On average, the most quiet sounds heard by people with their better ear are **between 70 and 95 dB**. People who suffer from severe hearing loss will benefit from powerful hearing aids, but often they rely heavily on lip-reading even when they are using hearing aids. Some also use sign language. |
| Profound hearing loss | On average, the most quiet sounds heard by people with their better ear are from **95 dB or more**. People who suffer from profound hearing loss are very hard of hearing and rely mostly on lip-reading, and/or sign language. |

Table 3.2: Audiometric descriptors and hearing loss according to the European Group on genetics of hearing impairments (EGGHI)

by the variability of different illnesses and test procedures, an abstraction of visual preferences of a person into three different profile groups concerning no, mild and moderate visual impairments was used (see table 3.3).

Regarding manual dexterity impairments, there are two ICF definitions available. B710 represents the functions of the range and ease of movement of a joint, focusing upon all different functions regarding the mobility of single joints. B730 concentrates upon the force generated by contraction of different muscles and muscle groups.

| Visual descriptors | Definitions of visual ability |
|---|---|
| No visual impairment | The subject does not use glasses and does not have any restrictions of visual ability. |
| Mild visual impairment | Mild visual impairments result in the use of glasses. Subject is slightly sensitive to light and glare, without glasses things appear to be indistinct or blurry and does have some minor problems to adjust to changes in light levels. |
| Moderate visual impairment | The user does have moderate impairments regarding vision. Glasses are necessary to see distant objects due to a moderate low visual acuity. |

Table 3.3: Separation of visual ability into three different profile groups

| Manual dexterity descriptors | Definitions of manual dexterity ability |
|---|---|
| No manual dexterity impairment | The subject does not have any restrictions regarding movement or force of joints. |
| Mild manual dexterity impairment | The subject does not have arthritis, but has slight problems when gripping small items and using small controls such as knobs, sliders, buttons or keys. |
| Moderate manual dexterity impairment | An early to intermediate phase of arthritis results in a moderate manual dexterity impairment of the user, who is not able to handle controls and items if they are too small. |

Table 3.4: Separation of manual dexterity ability into three different profile groups

Due to the variability of different manual dexterity diseases like Parkinson or Arthritis, a classification into different levels is necessary for further steps of User Model development. Table 3.4 shows the separation of manual dexterity impairments analogously into three different groups of no, mild and moderate impairments.

In terms of this thesis, each impairment was separated into three levels of no, mild and moderate. All different User Models are classified into these groups to ease the further step of abstraction for the inference of quantitative and qualitative recommendations.

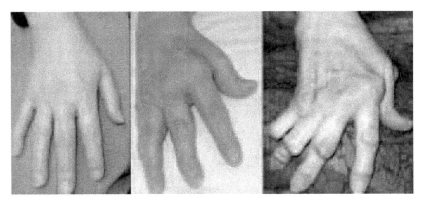

Figure 3.3: Hands affected by rheumatoid arthritis in early, intermediate and late phases (left to right, Source: Vicon Consortium [2010])

## 3.2.2 Methodology

In order to define problems of each target group related to impairment levels as presented in 3.2.1, the following methodology was carried out:

1. Introduction of the researcher and briefly to aims of this study. An introduction should give the subject a proper view of issues and topics.

2. Application and realization of each task.
   The subject performs different tasks with product. The tasks were predefined and describe a typical use.

3. After completion, a questionnaire was used to figure out problems related to impairments and functionalities.

In this step, some problematic areas could be identified while performing different tasks

4. In addition, the researcher records observations of each task to define how many participants have had problems with their task.
This is necessary for further observations and extraction of results that were not covered by the questionnaire.

### 3.2.3 Outcomes

Regarding this thesis, especially two outcomes were relevant. The identification of problematic issues while performing different tasks by the subjects resulted in textual recommendations for the designers. For further information see D1.1 of the VICON project (Vicon Consortium [2010]).

The other outcome is the separation of subjects into different profiles concerning their impairments and abilities. For each impairment of hearing, visual and manual dexterity, a classification into three profile groups was created using different preferences and parameter descriptions using nominal or categorical values of the subjects. The next chapter 3.3 will describe the attributes extracted from the user study for the creation of different Personas which were used for the inference and presentation of specific recommendations related to selections of designers of target User Models.

According to the definition of the reasoning process, in every step rules are used to define and classify different instances as members of different classes (e.g. User Model profiling). Also typical scenario settings to perform tasks using the product were extracted from the user study and will be described in chapter 3.4.

## 3.3 Virtual User Model

The main concept of Virtual User Models (VUM) is the representation of all scenario related issues in a knowledge base. In relation to this functionality, an Ontology was used to define classes and instances including a hierarchical taxonomy. In order to provide quantitative and qualitative recommendations (see 1.4) as an output of user specified parameters, various reasoning steps using forward-chain logic were implemented.

### 3.3.1 Knowledge Base

The knowledge base of the Virtual User Model was implemented using ontologies for each sub model. These models contain instances of User Models, Environments, Tasks, Components and Recommendations. Data properties, representing attributes for instances, were specified. The properties will be more granularly described in 3.3.2 for the User Model-, 3.3.3 for the Environment-, 3.3.4 for the Task-, 3.3.5 for the Component- and 3.3.6 for the Recommendation-related attributes.

To represent all data, an Ontology implementation was chosen due to aspects presented in 2.2. In summary this decision was endorsed by the following factors:

- Object oriented data structure
  An Ontology formally represents knowledge data including instances and relations. Each instance, e.g. User Model, can be related to different other classes and inherit various attributes like the age of a target user or if she or he needs glasses.

- Highly adaptable vocabulary
  In addition (or as a consequence) of the object oriented data structure, ontologies have the advantage to be highly adaptable to a problem by extending the Ontology vocabulary.

- Availability of reasoning
  Aside of the main purpose of the application of ontologies, reasoning is used to infer new states based upon initial models. These engines can be used to automate classification processes and decisions.

There are multiple Ontology frameworks on the market, with different pros and cons. For the realization of the knowledge base, Jena was used (see McBride [2002] and McBride [2001]) by concerning the following reasons.

- Adaptable interface
  The Jena Ontology framework offers a sophisticated Ontology interface with the advantage to manipulate all resources, predicates and values directly from within Java. With respect to the requirement of a server - client architecture, the server - implemented in Java - is able to perform manipulations of all Ontology instances.

- Inference support
  Jena contains a reasoning engine, which is able to operate with different sets of ontologies (RDF/S, OWL/lite, OWL/full). Also a very generic reasoner is included, which can also be manually extended by build-in rules.

## 3.3.2  User Model

The User Model represents the mass customization class of target users. Each user contains parameters and references to specific impairments, described either as nominal or abstract values. The used attributes were defined as an output of the user study.

| General characteristics | | |
|---|---|---|
| Predicate | Datatype | Description |
| Name | String | The name to identify a person is the only one primary predicate. Mandatory to define it in an instance |
| IDName | String | The IDname is unique for each object of the Ontology class. E.g. each user profile has a unique *IDName* assigned |
| Description | String | Description of the user profile or Persona represented by the profile |
| Nickname | String | Optional nickname for the person |
| VirtualModel | String | An URI (Uniform Resource Identifier, see Masinter et al. [2005]) where to find a virtual model e.g. in form of a wavefront .obj file format |
| Age | Integer (65-116) | Age in years |
| Gender | String (M or F) | Gender of person |

Table 3.5: Ontology class data properties used for User Model - General characteristics

The tables 3.5, 3.6, 3.7 and 3.8 present the different data properties of the User Model class. Each parameter can be used to define a specific User Model instance and will be used to classify the instance as a member of impairment groups.

In order to the output of recommendations, each User Model impairment group is resolved to emit different recommendations. The reasoning classifies each single User Model instance into separate impairment profiles (see section 3.4.4).

| Hearing | | |
|---|---|---|
| Predicate | Datatype | Description |
| Hearing500Hz | Integer (-10 - 120) | Threshold hearing level in dB at 500Hz (without aid) |
| Hearing1kHz | Integer (-10 - 120) | Threshold hearing level in dB at 1kHz (without aid) |
| Hearing2kHz | Integer (-10 - 120) | Threshold hearing level in dB at 2kHz (without aid) |
| Hearing4kHz | Integer (-10 - 120) | Threshold hearing level in dB at 4kHz (without aid) |
| SpeechWithBack-groundNoise | Integer (0 - 200%) | Threshold of speech intelligibility with background noise as percentage of background noise volume compared to speech volume |
| HearingAid | Integer (0 = No, 1 = Yes) | Indicator for worn hearing aid |
| HearingAidWith Product | Integer (0 = No, 1 = Yes) | Will the user wear hearing aid when using this kind of product? |

Table 3.6: Ontology class data properties used for User Model - Hearing

**Gandalf (80)**

*Gandalf is an active older gentleman who refuses to let his age stop him from do-ing things. He has a **moderate hearing loss** and **wears digital hearing aids all day long**. He **can follow conversa-tions in quiet places** without them but the aids make his life much easier. Due to his **moderate visual impairment** he wears his new **varifocal glasses** all of the time. **Moderate arthritis in both hands** does not stop him doing things but can cause him **discomfort**, especially in **cold weather**. So he **often wears gloves** in all seasons except the height of summer. Gandalf still drives a car and enjoys walk-ing his Labrador dog. He lives alone and tries to go to as many daytime social events as he can for company and enter-tainment.*

Figure 3.4: The "Gandalf" User Model (Source: Vicon Consortium [2012a])

| Vision | | |
|--------|--------|-------------|
| Predicate | Datatype | Description |
| VisualAcuity | Integer (0 = Normal, 1 = Mild, 2 = Moderate) | Visual acuity describes the "sharpness of vision"; value of normal = 20/12.5-20/25, mild = 20/32-20/63, moderate = 20/80-20/160 |
| FieldOfVision | Integer (0 = No, 1 = Slightly, 2 = Moderately, 3 = Strongly) | Reduced field of vision (finds it hard to see things to the side, top, bottom of what they are looking at) |
| Colour | Integer (0 = No, 1 = Yes) | Colour indicates if the user is colour blind |
| NearFocus | Integer (0 = No, 1 = Slightly, 2 = Moderately, 3 = Strongly) | Ability to clearly focus on objects at near distance (can be measured as Amplitude of Accommodation in centimetres) |
| DepthPerception | Integer (0 = Normal, 1 = Mild, 2 = Moderate) | Ability to judge distance |
| ContrastSensitivity | Integer ( 0 = Normal, 1 = Mild, 2 = Moderate) | Pelli-Robson Score as a measure of contrast sensitivity, value of normal = 1.6-2, mild = 1.1-1.5, moderate = 1.1-1.5 |
| Glare | Integer (0 = No, 1 = Yes) | Glare indicates if the user is sensitive to light and glare |
| Glasses | Integer (0 = No, 1 = Yes) | Indication if the user has glasses or contact lenses |
| GlassesWithProd-uct | Integer (0 = No, 1 = Yes) | Will the user wear glasses, or contact lenses, when using a product? |

Table 3.7: Ontology class data properties used for User Model - Vision

| Manual dexterity | | |
|---|---|---|
| Predicate | Datatype | Description |
| Arthritis | Integer (0 = No, 1 = Yes) | Answer to the question "Did the user report Arthritis?" |
| Grip | Integer (0 = No, 1 = Slightly, 2 = Moderately, 3 = Strongly) | Grip describes difficulty by holding small items, for example a pen or the handle of a cup, or items made of slippery material |
| Buttons | Integer (0 = No, 1 = Slightly, 2 = Moderately, 3 = Strongly) | Buttons estimates difficulty when using buttons or keys, for example when using the number keys on a phone |
| Discomfort | Integer (0 = No, 1 = Slightly, 2 = Moderately, 3 = Strongly) | Discomfort in hands when gripping small objects or operating controls |
| TouchSensitivity | Integer (0 = Normal, 1 = Mild, 2 = Moderate) | Sensitivity by touching different surfaces |

Table 3.8: Ontology class data properties used for User Model - Manual dexterity

"Gandalf" (see figure 3.4) represents an active elderly gentleman who is used as a representative for a specific target user group. Based upon textual issues presented in his description (bold marked), different abstract nominal and categorical values are extracted to form an analogue Ontology instance including different data properties.

| General characteristics | |
|---|---|
| Predicate | Value |
| Name | Gandalf |
| IDName | P5 |
| Description | Gandalf is an active older gentleman who refuses to let his age stop him from doing things.[...] |
| Nickname | N/A |
| VirtualModel | N/A |
| Age | 80 |
| Gender | M |

Continued on next page

| Hearing | |
|---|---|
| Predicate | Value |
| Hearing500Hz | 30 |
| Hearing1kHz | 45 |
| Hearing2kHz | 65 |
| Hearing4kHz | 75 |
| SpeechWithBackgroundNoise | 0 |
| HearingAid | 1 |
| HearingAidWithProduct | 1 |
| **Vision** | |
| Predicate | Value |
| VisualAcuity | 2 |
| FieldOfVision | 3 |
| Colour | 1 |
| NearFocus | 2 |
| DepthPerception | 2 |
| ContrastSensitivity | 2 |
| Glare | 1 |
| Glasses | 1 |
| GlassesWithProduct | 1 |
| **Manual dexterity** | |
| Predicate | Value |
| Arthritis | 1 |
| Grip | 3 |
| Buttons | 2 |
| Discomfort | 2 |
| TouchSensitivity | 2 |

Table 3.9: User Model definition for "Gandalf"

Using the inference model, the designer can select one single User Model "Gandalf", including different categorical and nominal values (see table 3.9), resulting in the output of all recommendations referring to impairment groups of the selected User Model instance.

As a pre-inference, the User Model "Gandalf" is classified into specific impairment profile groups so the system is able to connect the Persona to recommendation instances. Section 3.4.4 will present the reasoning in more detail.

All attributes (data properties) are also included in a cluster submission as part of the VUMS cluster Interoperable and Inclusive User Modelling concept for Simulation and Adaptation (Kaklanis et al. [2012a]) which deals as a definition which can be used by all VUMS projects: VERITAS (Chalkia et al. [2010]), VICON (Lawo et al. [2011]), GUIDE(Jung and Hahn [2011]) and MyUI (Strnad et al. [2012]).

### 3.3.3 Environment

The environment model is used to classify most-used environments to represent different aspects of environments (e.g. lighting levels) as nominal and abstract values. Each environment instance contains of different categorical or numerical values representing different aspects of an environment.

| General characteristics | | |
|---|---|---|
| Predicate | Datatype | Description |
| Name | String | The name to identify an environment is the only primary predicate. Mandatory to define it in an instance |
| IDName | String | The ID name is unique for each object of the Ontology class |
| Description | String | Textual description of the environment |
| RoomType | Integer (1 = Living room, 2 = Dining room, 3 = Kitchen, 4 = Living/dining room, 5 = Kitchen/dining room, 6 = Utility / storage room, 7 = Kitchen/dining/living room, 8 = Bathroom, 9 = Cellar, 10 = Other) | Room in which user trial took place |
| RoomWidth | Integer (1-99) | Estimate of room width (in meters) in which user trial took place |
| RoomLength | Integer (1-99) | Estimate of room length (in meters) in which user trial took place |

Continued on next page

| Door | Integer (1-999) | Number of doors in room where field trial took place |
|---|---|---|
| Window | Integer (1-999) | Number of windows in room where field trial took place |
| **Hearing** | | |
| Acoustics | Integer (1 = Good, 2 = Bad) | Acoustics in the room in which user trial took place |
| BackgroundNoise Level | Integer (0 = No background noise, 1 = Low, 2 = Loud) | Level of background noise in room in which user trial took place |
| BackgroundNoise Type | Integer (1 = TV/radio, 2 = People talking, 3 = Dog barking, 4 = Road works, 5 = Alarm, 6 = Traffic, 7 = Cooking appliance, 8 = Other household appliance, 9 = None) | Type of background noise in room in which user trial took place |
| **Vision** | | |
| LightingLevel | Integer ( 0 = Poor, 1 = Medium, 2= Bright) | Estimate of lighting level in room in which user trial took place |
| LightingType | Integer (1 = Natural lighting, 2 = Artificial lighting) | Estimate of type of lighting in room in which user trial took place |
| DirectLights | Integer (0 = No, 1 = Yes) | Existence of direct lights in the environment (direct lights and glossy surfaces are related to glare) |
| **Manual dexterity** | | |
| Temperature | Integer (0 = Cool, 1 = Comfortable, 3 = Warm) | Estimate of temperature level in room in which user trial took place |

Continued on next page

| | | |
|---|---|---|
| WMClearSpace Front | Integer (1-999) | Amount of clear space (in cm) in front of the washing machine |
| WMClearSpace Left | Integer (1-999) | Amount of clear space (in cm) at the left of the washing machine |
| WMClearSpace Right | Integer (1-999) | Amount of clear space (in cm) at the right of the washing machine |

Table 3.10: Ontology class data properties used for Environment

Environment instances are created using outcomes of the user study (see section 3.2). Each environment refers to a different surrounding of the user in his or her daily life. Using these abstract representation, the system is able to recommend design guides based upon the specific surroundings. All environment-related recommendations are connected to environment instances directly by a specified *EnvRule* parameter of each recommendation which defines when a single recommendation should be presented (see a more detailed review in section 3.3.6 and 3.4.4).

## 3.3.4 Task

The task class represents one specific task which the beneficiaries can perform using the product. Each task refers to a different set of recommendations.

| General characteristics | | |
|---|---|---|
| Predicate | Datatype | Description |
| Name | String | Name of the task is presented to the user in the UI |
| IDName | String | The ID name is unique for each object of the Ontology class |
| Nr | Integer (1-999) | The task number identification code, unique for every task |
| Description | String | Textual description of the task |
| Impairment | String | Each impairment profile can be defined here as in recommendation class as comma-separated values for impairment groups for direct connection (see table 3.13) |
| Component | String | Specific component name involved in a task (see Component Model) |

Continued on next page

| Complexity | Integer (0 = Not complex, 1 = Medium complex, 2 = Severe) | The complexity estimate of a task |
|---|---|---|
| InputRequired | Integer (0 = No, 1 = Yes) | Identifies if an input to the task object is required |
| Input | String | Input character chain, if required (can be extended to regular expression describing the input) |
| InputDescription | String | Optional textual description of the input |
| NumberOf Subtasks | Integer (1-99) | Number of subtasks the task is composed of |
| Subtasks | String | Hierarchically numbered list of subtasks. The numbering scheme is as follows <Number>.<SubtaskNumber>, e.g. 2.4 for the fourth subtask of the task number two. The subtasks in the list are separated by comma. |

Table 3.11: Ontology class data properties used for Task

These abstract values are used to represent an abstract relation between the tasks and the problems if the target user fulfils this task. The recommendation definition of the *TaskRule* attribute (see table 3.13) of each recommendation connects each recommendation to a specific task (see 3.3.6 and 3.4.4 for a detailed review).

### 3.3.5 Component

The component model is used in the CAD phase of the project. It defines the annotation options during the annotation step in the CAD module. Each component refers to a different set of recommendations which can also be optionally applied to a CAD object.

| General characteristics | | |
|---|---|---|
| Predicate | Datatype | Description |
| Name | String | The annotated component name, will be presented in the CAD Annotation Form |
| State | String | How many states can the component perform (e.g. switch with 2 states) |
| Function | String | Description of the functionality of each component (e.g. binary state change for "press button") |

Table 3.12: Ontology class data properties used for Component

As already mentioned, a CAD module in Siemens NX was implemented. Using the module, the designer is able to view recommendations for the current prototype but also applies rules like e.g. "The minimum size of a button for visual impaired users is $1cm^2$". These "quantitative" recommendations, as defined in 1.4, always refer to a specific component of the prototype (see 4.2.3 for a detailed review).

## 3.3.6 Recommendation

The recommendation class defines the presented output of the system for the user. Both qualitative and quantitative recommendations (see 1.4) can be represented.

| General characteristics | | |
|---|---|---|
| Predicate | Datatype | Description |
| Name | String | The recommendation name will be presented in the "Select Recommendation" Form |
| Priority | Integer (1 = Low, 2 = Middle, 3 = High) | The importance level of one recommendation. High priority means that the recommendation is a "MUST HAVE" |
| Summary | String | An optional summary of a recommendation |
| Text | String | The complete text of a guideline recommendation |

Continued on next page

| Source | String | The source of a recommendation (e.g. ISO Guideline or experience) |
|---|---|---|
| Attachment | String | An URI (Uniform Resource Identifier, see Masinter et al. [2005]), where an attachment can be found |
| Profile | String | The profile or profiles of a recommendation used for the rules. 6 profiles are available: VI1 and VI2 for mild and moderate visual impairment profiles; HI1 and HI2 for mild and moderate hearing impairments; MD1 and MD2 for mild and moderate hearing impairments. The level of no impairment can be defined an empty String ("") |
| EnvRule | String | The rule with Jena inference syntax, if a recommendation should be presented, related to environment selection of the user, i.e. $le(?lighting\_level, 2)$ |
| TaskRule | String | The rule with Jena inference syntax related to task selection of the user, if a recommendation should be presented |
| Component | String | A component name of recommendation directly related to a specific component (e.g. "Button") |
| ComponentRule | String | The rule with Jena inference syntax, if a recommendation should be presented, related to component functionalities and attributes |
| Phase | Integer (1 = Sketch, 2 = CAD, 3 = Evaluation) | Application Phase definition, when a recommendation should be presented |

Table 3.13: Ontology class data properties used for Recommendation

Each recommendation represents one specific suggestion for designers, how a product can be developed for a specific target user group. By using the *EnvRule* or *TaskRule*, different rules can be defined using the Jena inference syntax, by which input selection of the designer a specific task should be presented.

The "Phase" attribute refers to the specific product development phase, when a recommendation is relevant. In this thesis only the Sketch and CAD phases are focused.

## 3.4 Reasoning

A reasoning step is needed to infer from available data information. As presented in the previous chapter all relevant recommendations to the user are based upon a predefined setting. This section deals with the syntax used for the realisation and presents the complete reasoning approach. The Jena framework used here includes a general purpose rule-based reasoner (henceforth referred to as generic rule reasoner) which is able to apply rules to the current Ontology state with the output of a new state.

### 3.4.1 Rules

| *Rule* | := *bare-rule* . |
| | or [ *bare-rule* ] |
| | or [ ruleName : *bare-rule* ] |
| *bare-rule* | := *term*, ... *term* ->*hterm*, ... *hterm* // forward rule |
| | or *bhterm* <- *term*, ... *term* // backward rule |
| *hterm* | := *term* |
| | or [ *bare-rule* ] |
| *term* | := (*node, node, node*) // triple pattern |
| | or (*node, node, functor*) // extended triple pattern |
| | or builtin(*node, ... node*) // invoke procedural primitive |
| *bhterm* | := (*node, node, node*) // triple pattern |
| *functor* | := functorName(*node, ... node*) // structured literal |
| *node* | := uri-ref // e.g. http://foo.com/eg |
| | or prefix:localname // e.g. rdf:type |

Table 3.14: Informal description of the simplified text rule syntax of reasoner (Source: The Apache Software Foundation [2013])

Rules are used to infer from one state and setting to new states by application of rule sets. For instance all User Models are classified into impairment groups using predefined rules. These rules classify each instance of User Models by data values as presented in tables 3.5-3.8 into different impairment groups.

Table 3.14 presents an informal description of the rule syntax of the reasoning[1]. Regarding the purpose of this thesis, to get new information from the initial Ontology model including User Models, environments etc. forward chain logic rules were implemented. These rules represent different parametrical thresholds to add a new membership for single Ontology instances to each model, if the parameters match the rule set.

For instance the rule:

| Rule | Description |
|---|---|
| (?x rdf:type Vicon:UserModel), | For each instance of the class Vicon:UserModel |
| (?x Vicon:UserModelArthritis ?artritis), equal(?arthritis,"Y") | Creation of the variable ?artritis Check if the value of the parameter is "Y" |
| ->(?x rdf:type Vicon:UsersWithArthritis). | Resulting inference, here a new membership is added |

infers all User Model instances, which have a "Y" as value of the "UserModelArtritis" parameter as members of the class "Vicon:UsersWithArtritis". This scheme of rules is used for all models (for more detailed information about the RETE algorithm itself, see Forgy [1982] and Shrobe [1993]).

The complete reasoning of the framework can be seen as a sequence of Ontology model inferences with the result of new classes.

## 3.4.2  Reasoning Engine

Figure 3.5 presents the complete reasoning process for the final Ontology. Based upon the initial Ontology, as shown in the previous section, the process contains five inferences up to the final model. The first inference classifies User Model instances using different rules according to WHO ICF user profiles (see Organization et al. [2012a] and Organization et al. [2012b]). With respect to the Ontology model, this step adds new memberships for each User Model to different, already created profile classes. These classes are separated into no impairments (e.g. HProfile0 for no hearing impairment group), mild (e.g. VProfile1 for mild visual impairment group) and moderate (e.g. MDProfile2 for moderate manual dexterity impairment group) levels for visual, manual dexterity and hearing impairments. The second inference deals with component recommendations, resulting in analogue new classes with member instances for each recommendation related to an annotated component. These rec-

---

[1]Complete syntax description can be found at http://jena.apache.org/documentation/inference/

ommendations will be presented in the CAD phase. The last three steps deal with the immediate textual recommendations presented in the sketch phase regarding the selection of the designer of a User Model, typical environment and typical task.

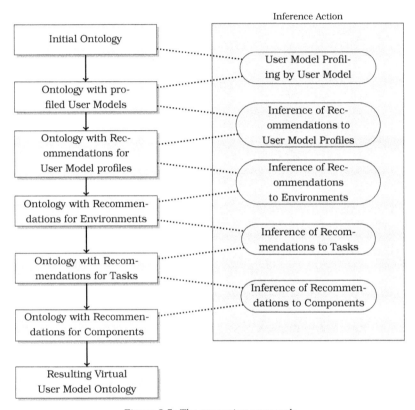

Figure 3.5: The reasoning approach

### 3.4.3 Reasoning Approach

As previously mentioned, the VICON reasoning consists of several stages in the creation of the final Virtual User Model. In the first stage, based upon a user study [Vicon Consortium, 2010] User Model instances are added as members to impairment groups.

To simplify the reasoning the user can add or change rules directly. The syntax was reduced so that predicate values of instances are already assigned. The user can use them without a definition. For each step single files are applied, so the variable generation could be automatically produced, if the name of the variable is the same[1] as the attribute name defined in class properties. For instance if the variable *?visualacuity* is used, the definition *(?x Vicon:UserModelVisualAcuity ?visualacuity)* is added to the term.

Each of predicate value can be compared using the syntax presented in Table 3.14.

Each User Model instance is classified by parameter values. For instance the classification of mild manual dexterity impaired user groups is made using the following rule:

"equal(?arthritis,"N"), equal(?grip,2), equal(?controls,2), equal(?buttons,2), equal(?discomfort,2) -> (?x rdf:type Vicon:MDProfile1)."

By using build-in commands like "equal(x,y)", values are compared to each other. The right arrow defines the state, if all axioms are true (forward chaining). Usually all variables (starting with a "?") must be defined first before the first comparison. For instance, to get the value of the predicate, if the User Model suffers from arthritis, the first axioms should be: "(?x rdf:type Vicon:UserModel),(?x Vicon:UserModelArthritis ?arthritis) [...]"

In the first axiom, an instance of the User Model class is selected ("?x"). The value of the arthritis predicate (analogue other predicates) can be set afterwards by using the direct predicate name, always beginning with "Vicon" and the class name. All stages of reasoning are compiled analogue to this scheme resulting in new inference models until the final Virtual User Model.

Using the knowledge base as initial model, a new model is deducted including new classes for the separation of selection states. While the knowledge base is defined as a flat hierarchy, the inference Ontology contains a tree-based taxonomy for the recommendation model.

1. Classify "User Model" instances to user profiles (mass customization, see also Pine and Davis [1999]):
   This first reasoning step will be needed to define different profiles based upon the possibilities and user needs of the beneficiaries.

2. Add recommendations to each User Model profile class as members:
   After this step, recommendations can be connected to User Models.

3. Add recommendations to each environment class as members:
   Thus each environment instance is an instance and cannot contain members,

---

[1]Comparison is made in lower case

as a pre-step each instance needs to have an analogue class where members can be applied.

4. Add recommendations to each task class as members:
   This step is analogue to the previous environment step, involving all recommendations having an impact on specific task selections of the user.

5. Add recommendations to each component class as members:
   This step deals with the presentation of recommendations for the second phase CAD, where based upon annotations of the components of the virtual prototype different recommendations should be presented.

## 3.4.4 Ontology Inference

The Forward Chain Reasoning steps of the Ontology create new classes. Exemplary rules were used to create new User Model classes for each specified hearing impairment group.

```
1  //HI0
2  lessThan(?hearing500hz, 20) , lessThan(?hearing1khz, 25), lessThan(?
       hearing2khz,30), lessThan(?hearing4khz,40),
3  greaterThan(?backgroundnoise,100)
4  -> (?x rdf:type VICON:HProfile0).
5  //HI1
6  equal(?hearing500hz, 20) , equal(?hearing1khz, 25), equal(?
       hearing2khz,30), equal(?hearing4khz,40),
7  equal(?backgroundnoise,100)
8  -> (?x rdf:type VICON:HProfile1).
9  //HI2
10 equal(?hearing500hz, 30) , equal(?hearing1khz, 45), equal(?
       hearing2khz,65), equal(?hearing4khz,75),
11 equal(?backgroundnoise,0)
12 -> (?x rdf:type VICON:HProfile2).
```

Figure 3.6: Recommendation Rules to create User Model Recommendation for impaired groups

Figure 3.6 presents e.g. rules, which were used to add a new membership[1] to each User Model instance based on their predicates, which are related to hearing impairments. As mentioned in 3.3.2, these predicates define targeted WHO ICF impairment groups. After the reasoning step, new classes are created (e.g. *HProfile1* for mild hearing impaired target users) describing a classification of each User Model by

---

[1]For instance a membership of an instance to the User Model class is defined by *(?x rdf:type Vicon:UserModel)*

| Predicate | Value |
|---|---|
| Name | For better tactility keys should be raised above the body of the phone |
| Profile | VI1,VI2,MD1,MD2 |
| Summary | Keys should be raised above the body of the phone (preferably by 5 mm). |
| ID | R-5 |
| Source | NCBI, http://www.cardiac-eu.org/guidelines/keys.htm, http://www.cardiac-eu.org/guidelines/telecoms/mobile.htm |
| ComponentRule | button_height $\geq$ 5 |
| Component | turning knob, press button |
| Text | People who rely on touch to operate keypads benefit from keys that are as distinctive as possible to the touch. Raised keys are more easily distinguished than those that are flush against their surrounding. Keys should therefore be raised above the body of the phone (preferably by 5 mm). |
| Level | 3 |

Table 3.15: One instance of the recommendation class

defined parameters.

Analogue steps are performed for the classification of visual and manual dexterity impairments.

For the classification of recommendations to each selection of the user, instances contain values to connect with various classes. Table 3.15 presents one instance of the recommendation class including all defined attributes[1]. With respect to the purpose of defining recommendations based on different selections of the user, each instance contains information about target User Models, Environment Models, Task Models and Component Models.

- User Model
  The impact between one recommendation instance and their importance to different impairments is described in the "Profile" predicate.

- Task
  The *TaskRule* predicate is used to describe the relation between tasks and rec-

[1] 87 recommendation instances available in total.

ommendation instances. On task side, each instance can optionally contain a direct connection to the profile predicate of the recommendation class by the *Impairment* predicate in which recommendations are presented, if the same impairment profile groups are included (see task parameters, table 3.11).

- Environment
  The *EnvRule* predicate represents the connection between environment and recommendation instances.

- Component
  For the component relation, available annotation component options are specified in the "Component" predicate.

## 3.4.5 Description Logic Expressivity

Description Logic (DL) expressivity denotes the complexity of operators used throughout the Ontology (Baader [2003]). Table 3.16 presents the expressivity used by the Ontology.

| Naming convention | Description |
|---|---|
| **AL** | Attributive language. This is the base language which allows: <br> • Atomic negation (negation of concept names that do not appear on the left hand side of axioms) <br> • Concept intersection <br> • Universal restrictions <br> • Limited existential quantification |
| **C** | Complex concept negation. |
| **H** | Role hierarchy (sub properties - rdfs:subPropertyOf). |
| **(D)** | Use of data type properties, data values or data types. |

Table 3.16: Used DL Expressivity of Ontology

The initial model applies the DL expressivity with role hierarchy expressions especially for a hierarchical structure of recommendations and data type properties for attribute values of instances (e.g. parameter *UserModelAge* with an integer value as seen in tables 3.5-3.8). The complexity of the final resulting model after the inference of rules is defined by **ALCH(D)**.

### 3.4.6 Multiple Selection

In the final application, the designer can select multiple User Models, environments and tasks, resulting in a set of recommendations. In the initial set of recommendations, each one refers to one User Model impairment profile, typical environment or task setting. With respect to section 1.3 and 3.4.4, each selection of the designer results in a specific set of recommendations. For instance, if the designer selects the User Model "Gandalf", the presented recommendations are members of each impairment profile class, which the User Model "Gandalf" is classified to. Each presented recommendation has an impact on a specific impairment profile (e.g. class of moderate hearing impaired). A combined set is created containing all recommendations for each impairment group. If the user selects more than one User Model, the recommendations for all must be merged.

An intersection of the different sets would result in an empty set, due to the connection of each recommendation to different aspects.

## 3.5 Conclusion

This chapter presented a knowledge modelling approach to include relevant data into a knowledge base. Based on chapter 2 context modelling structures were compared with respect to different requirements and led to the conclusion, that especially Ontology based models (see section 3.1) are suitable with respect to requirements of partial validation, level of formality and applicability to existing environments as an answer to hypothesis 1.

**Hypothesis 1 (*Ontology based model application*)**

> Ontology based models can be used to store and manipulate various data concerning requirements especially of elderly people for the use of products.

Various models (e.g. User Model) were structured based on a user study with beneficiaries resulting in a definition for each part. User Model, Environment Model, Task Model, Component Model and Recommendation Model were defined and combined for scenario representation. The combination (Virtual User Model) including reasoning is able to connect recommendations by input selection of target beneficiary group, typical environment in which the product can be used and typical task.

# Chapter 4

# Application in Development Process

The following chapter focuses upon the application of the knowledge base presented in the previous chapter in a development process. Using inclusive design guidelines, personal expertise of designers and user studies, an Ontology was defined including recommendations. All resulting data including context information and recommendations (qualitative and quantitative, see section 3.3.6) use graphical front end applications and an integrated module in CAD software.

## 4.1 System architecture

This section deals with the application part of the system giving a general overview, required tools were developed. A software back end facilitates this.

### 4.1.1 Overview

Figure 4.1 shows the system architecture with the different applications. The approach consists of a socket server representing the Ontology interface for sketch and CAD product development phases and the backend Ontology.

In accordance with the proposed Virtual User Model a software framework has been implemented as a core part of the support system. The aim of this framework is to support designers in a non-obstructive way during the product development.

In the first phase designers create draft sketches of the target product. This step can include different software solutions, but with respect to requirements of designers they often create these drafts on paper sheets. Therefore a stand alone solution

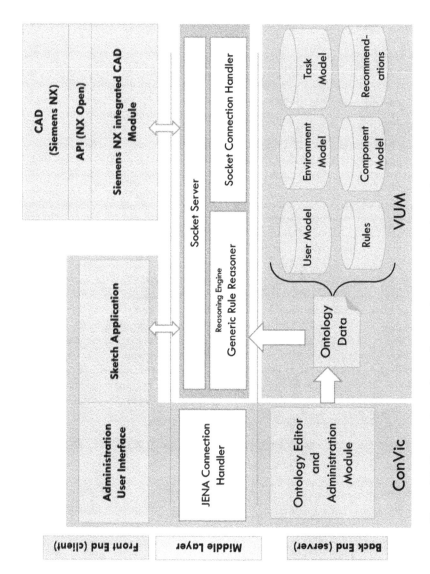

Figure 4.1: The complete software framework containing back- and front end applications

was desired. The resulting recommendations are exported for later use in following design phases.

The software application called ConVic is used in this phase and consists of two different front ends. The sketch application front end (see section 4.2.1) presents an interface to the designer to get qualitative recommendations based on different user input scenarios. For maintenance, manipulation and extension purposes of the VUM before reasoning, an administrator interface directly communicates with the Ontology using a connection handler as a middle layer. ConVic connects to the Ontology in the back end (left side of figure 4.1). Also the sketch application, included in the ConVic, connects to the Ontology using a socket server middle layer. In this middle layer the reasoning is implemented as presented in section 3.4 to access the VUM after reasoning. This separation of both connection types (before and after reasoning) was necessary due to the reasoning steps. The socket server provides access to the final construct, the administration module to the initial model.

In this first step a VSF (Vicon Status File, see 4.1.4) is created for export including the current input scenario selection of the designer. It can be imported in the integrated CAD module. This is used in the second phase (CAD) in which designers create objects in a virtual environment including simple boxes, spheres, cubes etc. without specific functional context. With respect to the aim to support the designer, functionality of a component must be annotated previously (see 4.2.3). The Component Model defines all currently available functional types (see 3.3.5) to get qualitative and quantitative recommendations for each annotated CAD object and is used in the annotation tab of the CAD module. So the designer can set up context to the model. Afterwards the CAD module provides a set of recommendations based on annotation selections. This can also be applied directly by the module if it is a quantitative recommendation.

To summarize, the framework includes the following applications and services:

- Administration User Interface:
  The Administration User Interface provides different tools to change and manipulate the initial Ontology and rule sets. Also the Sketch Application is included for preview purposes of the final VUM.

- Sketch Application:
  This application connects to the socket server and provides an interface to display different recommendations based on the selections of user profile, typical environment and typical task

- CAD (Siemens NX):
  Siemens NX is used as a CAD software solution for the approach presented in this thesis

- API (NX Open):
  Siemens NX includes an API called NX Open to access the virtual environment which is used to read and manipulate all virtual objects.

- Siemens NX integrated CAD module:
  The CAD module connects to the Socket Server to provide different support to designers while creating and manipulating a product in CAD Software Siemens NX.

- JENA Connection Handler:
  The Handler is used for the direct connection to the Ontology by parsing and translating commands into SPARQL to access the Ontology (Prud'Hommeaux et al. [2008]). Equal commands are also implemented in the Socket Connection Handler

- Socket Server:
  This part of the software is not visible to the end users (designers). It provides a middle-layer between all applications to the Ontology data.

- Generic Rule Reasoner:
  Using the reasoner, inferred from the initial Ontology the final construct is created as presented in 3.4.

- Socket Connection Handler:
  Similar as the JENA Connection Handler, this part parses and translates commands as "get users" into an equivalent SPARQL command to access parameters and data properties of each model (Prud'Hommeaux et al. [2008]).

- Ontology Editor and Administration Module:
  Using SPARQL commands generated by the JENA Connection Handler, this module also uses JENA to read and manipulate the Ontology data directly (Prud'Hommeaux et al. [2008]).

- Ontology Data, User Model, Environment Model, Task Model, Component Model, Rules and Recommendations:
  This part represents the initial model which is used for the reasoning. All context related data is already included.

For usability purposes and especially regarding acceptance of designers, a software installer is provided to install all parts of the framework. During the installation process and in case Siemens NX is already installed, it creates a new user role and all necessary registry values in which the CAD module is included in the toolbar of Siemens NX.

## 4.1.2  User Input

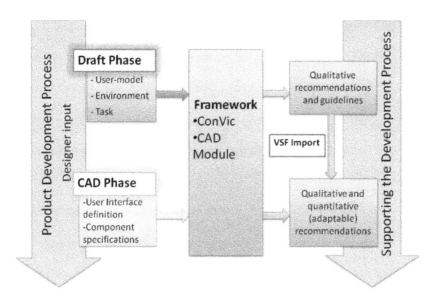

Figure 4.2: User input of the designer supporting the sketch design and
CAD phases of Product Development Process

Figure 4.2 presents a functional diagram concerning the input of designers and the output of the framework. As previously mentioned (see 2.1), designers create sketches using paper drafts or software solutions. To maintain a flexible support, a stand alone application was implemented (**ConVic**). Hereby, designers can select different possible scenarios in which the target product can be used, resulting in qualitative (see 1.4) textual design recommendations. A multi-selection of scenarios is also possible, representing the use of the product by different impairment groups, in different typical environments, performing different typical tasks and resulting in a merged set of recommendations for all scenarios (see also 3.4.6).

In the CAD phase, software applications (CAD/CAE/CAx) are used for the creation of a virtual prototype. With respect to the design process and the requirement of an as un-obstructive system as possible, an integrated module in Siemens NX was implemented. The user input in this phase is the virtual product itself, which is designed simultaneously while using the module.

Virtual environments focus upon the representation of physical attributes and surfaces, most often ignoring functional issues. It is necessary to set up each component and add context and type related attributes by the user. Regarding this issue, an annotation tool as a part of the CAD module was implemented, by which the designer is able to annotate e.g. a cube as a press button. Using this functional annotation, for each component a set of recommendations is presented (qualitative or quantitative) which should be considered. Quantitative recommendations, as presented in 1.4, contain limits of parameters (e.g. minimum button label size) of interface components. To support the designer, these parameters can also be applied directly to the virtual component, if the parameter mentioned is defined.

### 4.1.3  Server Tool

All connections between the back end and all front end applications are implemented by the Socket Server Application middleware, which provides reasoning using JENA(McBride [2002]) and commands to get all instances and relations between instances from the Ontology. ConVic includes a JENA-based interface to the Ontology (Ontology Editor and Administration Utilities) and also the Sketch Application, which can be started separately, for preview purposes (Vicon Consortium [2011b] described these interfaces (section 3) as back end and front end). Each of the front end applications Sketch Design Application, Administrator Software, CAD Modules and Interfaces and the Virtual Reality Simulation Platform uses data, which is provided by the Socket Server. For each product (mobile phone, washing machine and TV remote) the server creates a different port (65000 for mobile phone, 65001 for washing machine and 65002 for TV remote) on the server and provides all relevant information through commands.

The Socket Server is included in the setup file as an applicable Java JAR. This JAR file contains all relevant information of the back end and the middleware itself. To start it on the current machine, it is just necessary to run the JAR file. This software component deals with direct communications between the client and the server side and requires ports 65000 to 65002 to be open. Manipulation is possible using the administration software.

```
1   <?xml version="1.0" encoding="UTF-8" ?>
2   <Phase1>
3       <UserModel>
4           Gandalf
5       </UserModel>
6       <Environment>
7           Cellar
8       </Environment>
9       <Task>
10          Check wash dial
11      </Task>
12  </Phase1>
13  <Phase2>
14      <CADFilename>
15          Arcelik_WashingMachine.stp
16      </CADFilename>
17  </Phase2>
```

Figure 4.3: VSF Manifest.xml example file providing the selections of the designer

### 4.1.4 Vicon Status Files

The Vicon Status File (VSF) is used regarding intercommunication between the phase specific applications. In the first phase, the designer creates a product as a draft, getting textual qualitative recommendations to consider ensuring inclusive design. These recommendations are also relevant for the second phase software, in which the user creates a virtual prototype of the same draft product. Vicon Status File can be used to represent the setting from the first phase to the second phase.

Vicon Status Files are containers including documents or other files. Each VSF contains one main file "Manifest.xml", which describes the selection, which is already made in a previous stage of product development.

Figure 4.3 presents an exemplary Manifest.xml file defining information about the first phase concerning a selection of the User Model "Gandalf", the environment "Cellar" and the task "Check wash dial". Using these selections in the second phase module, recommendations can be applied which were already presented in the first phase software. The VSF for the transfer between the second and the third phase

```
1   <?xml version="1.0" encoding="utf-8"?>
2   <Product>
3        <ComponentList>
4            <Component type="PressButton" id="button_on">
5                <LocalPosition x="0.01455851" y="0.04557789" z
                    ="0.009" />
6                <LocalRotation x="0" y="0" z="0" />
7                <Dimension x="0.014" y="0.007375001" z="0.002" />
8                <Color r="0" g="0" b="0" />
9                <MinimumForce>28</MinimumForce>
10               <PressDepth>0.2</PressDepth>
11               <Component type="Text" id="button_on_text">
12                   <LocalPosition x="0" y="0" z="0.001" />
13                   <LocalRotation x="0" y="0" z="0" />
14                   <Dimension x="0.014" y="0.007375001" z="0.0001"
                        />
15                   <Color r="1" g="1" b="1" />
16                   <FontSize>12</FontSize>
17               </Component>
18           </Component>
19           [...]
20       </ComponentList>
21       <Information>
22           <Name>Doro 332gsm</Name>
23           <Type>Cell Phone</Type>
24           <Vendor>Doro</Vendor>
25           <OntologyServer ip="xxx.xxx.xxx.xxx" port="65000"/>
26       </Information>
27   </Product>
```

Figure 4.4: VSF meta.xml example file providing the annotations of component parameters

79

also contain the model file, which was used in the CAD software (see "CADFilename" tag in Figure 4.3). Additionally to the Manifest.xml, from the second to the third phase, a "meta.xml" file is included in the VSF.

The "meta.xml" file provides all meta information regarding the model and product components (see figure 4.4). Each object in the virtual environment is added, including the annotation (type of a component), the current id and the file name of the CAD model, which is also included in the VSF container. Physical data as local positioning of components are automatically included. VSF containers including the three files: "Manifest.xml", "meta.xml" and the corresponding model file are used for the transition from second to third phase.

## 4.2 Tools

This section describes all front end applications included in the development of a product. Both tools support designers by providing recommendations for the target product.

### 4.2.1 Sketch Design Tool

**Overview**

The Sketch Design tool (see figure 4.5) will support the first design step (phase 1: sketch design phase). The system uses a choice of a User Model (Persona), an environment and a task.

The output of the application is a number of textual recommendations and attached files (e.g. specific templates for graphic design software). The Sketch Design tool is distributed as an applicable JAR file included in the installation setup. To start the application, it is necessary to start the JAR file.

The Sketch Design tool includes the following specific functionality:

- Device selection (mobile phone, washing machine or TV remote)

- Selection of User Model (Persona), typical environments and typical tasks

- Output of textual recommendations

- List of recommendations

- Export current list of recommendations as RTF or PDF

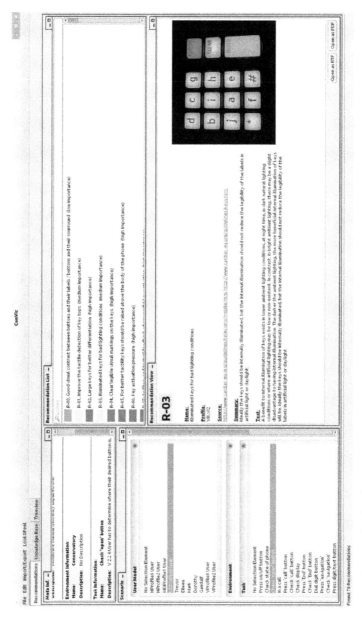

Figure 4.5: Sketch Design application. On the left the user is able to select User Models, typical Environments and typical Tasks. A multiple selection is also possible.

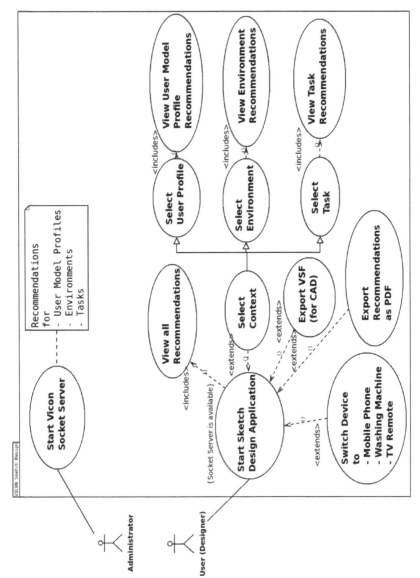

Figure 4.6: Use-case diagram (UML) of the Sketch Design application.

### Product development workflow

The work flow of figure 4.6 demonstrates the support of the system in relation to user input for the role models administrative user and designer. The Socket Server needs to be available as middleware (see Vicon Consortium [2011b]) for the designer to be able to use or to have access to the Ontology data. It provides an interface for the selections of User Model profiles, typical environment settings and typical tasks.

After the designer started the Sketch Design Application, she or he can set up the target device type for the product development. By selecting a user profile, environment and task, recommendations are presented to the user. The user is also able to export the current set of recommendations to a PDF file for later analysis and printing purposes. Also the selections can be exported into a VSF, which can be imported in the CAD phase for the presentation of recommendations from the sketch design phase.

## 4.2.2  Administration Tool

### Overview

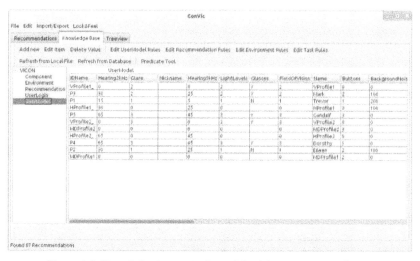

Figure 4.7: Knowledge base interface of the Administration software

The Administration Tool **ConVic** is distributed as an applicable JAR file and is included in the installation setup. To start the application, it is necessary to run the JAR file (with Java installed) using the Start menu of Windows. It also includes the Socket Server and requires the ports 65000 to 65002 to be open.

ConVic consists of three parts, which can be chosen by a tab panel. The *Recommendations* tab presents the Sketch Design View on the Ontology (see next section). After all changes of the Ontology, a restart is required (File → Restart) to update this view.

To change the Ontology, e.g. if you want to add new Recommendations, the *Knowledge Base* presents an interface to all classes, which are used to build the reasoning part (see figure 4.7). The administrator can select the Ontology class on the left and modify the Ontology class on the right. Each class is presented as a table including all instances and predicates. It also contains the following functionality:

- Rule editor to change all rule sets

- Predicate tool to change variables and attributes of a class

- Repository interface to connect with a MySQL server for version support of the Ontology and rules

- Add, edit and delete instances of all classes

- Import of all different class instances from Comma-Separated-Values (Excel CSV) File

- Export of the Ontology File (OWL) after reasoning

The TreeView (last tab) visualizes the Ontology after reasoning in a tree-based design. The right side of the TreeView provides a legend and an orientation control frame. Additionally by holding the right mouse button and moving the mouse forward / backward the perspective zooms in / out of the TreeView.

Administrators are able to add new instances to each class by using the "Add new Instances" dialogue in the knowledge base view. A description for the predicates is presented too. The Predicate Tool of the Administration software provides the feature to change the predicates of each Ontology class. VUMS Cluster XML files can be imported and exported directly to the Ontology.

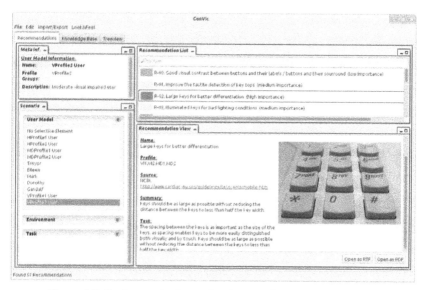

Figure 4.8: Designer role view with selection of VProfile2 User Model

**Product development workflow**

Using the Administration software component, the designer is able to get recommendations based upon selections and to change the complete Ontology. This software is directly used by the designers in the evaluation.

In the Sketch Design phase, the administrator role needs to provide a Socket Server on local or remote system. Afterwards the designer role can start the sketch application to connect to the server system.

Figure 4.8 presents the selection of moderate visual impaired users. The presented recommendations only concentrate upon all factors and user needs related to "VProfile2" User Model, as defined in Vicon Consortium [2012a].

### 4.2.3 CAD Module

**Overview**

During the CAD design phase designers use commercial CAD software. In the VI-CON project Siemens NX e.g. was used (see Vicon Consortium [2010a] and Vicon Consortium [2010b]). In order to push the sketch-phase recommendations to the CAD system, a software module using NX's API toolkit has been developed. Siemens modelling environment has a collection of API toolkits called NX Open. NX Open allows access and manipulation of models designed with NX as well as customization of the NX user interface to suit individual needs. The "Common API" toolkit compatible with the requirements as defined in Vicon Consortium [2011a] exposes the same object model for a number of programming languages (Java, C#, etc.). A comprehensive understanding of the core concepts such as how the API exposes objects within NX is necessary. It is an advantage that the common API gives access to the same object model used by NX developers.

Extensive interfaces can be established with the modelling environment. The elements of the object model are semantically incomplete. Modelling environment concentrates upon primary visual and surface parameters, functional parameters are not included. Siemens NX offers the possibility to add custom parameters, which does not need to be related to current components. These attributes are stored within the component and can be used to represent functional parameter values like the force needed to push a button. Additionally these values can be set and reset automatically by recommendations (e.g. to minimum values).

With respect to the analysis of the product design processes (on behalf of industrial partners) and the expectations provided by respective designers and developers it turned out to be a basic requirement that the shape of a product (and / or its user interface) should not become "dictated" by a recommendation system. Moreover, designers usually prefer to start with sketches and drawings on paper from scratch. In order to achieve this, the system provides templates for component names that can be imported into an existing product model. This way the product developer has the alternative either to compare his own model with the loaded component templates or to use the template according to his ideas. In other words, in order to support creativity for the product developers, parameters and dimensions of a CAD model are only manipulated within the predefined templates.

The utilization of component templates provides a further advantage that the geometrical dimensions of the components can be reduced to a subset of core param-

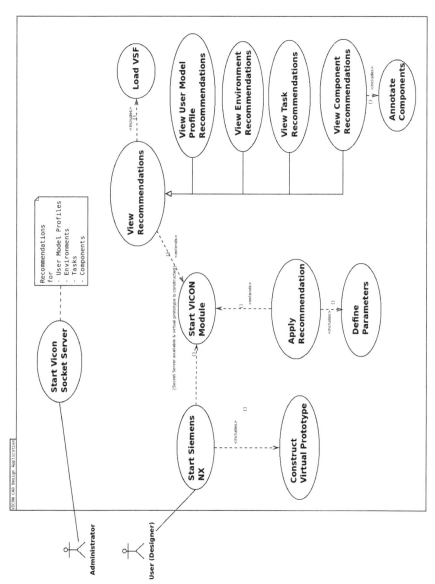

Figure 4.9: Use-case diagram (UML) of the CAD module.

eters. For instance, an external parameter such as "recommended button size" can be used in context of defining a keypad with round buttons and in parallel a keypad with square buttons.

The final prototype will not provide a complete set of templates, but the templates for the most typical components such as keypads, displays, etc. used in mobile phones, washing machines and TV remotes. Additionally, the user has the possibility of defining own customized templates supported by the core parameters that are provided by the recommendation system.

**Product development workflow**

The integration of inclusive design into the CAD process was developed as a module within Siemens NX. The user (designer) is able to connect to the socket server and to get support by visual recommendations. Recommendations can be directly applied to objects. Figure 4.9 presents the use case diagram for this phase. Analogue to the sketch design phase, the module needs a Socket Server available to access all relevant data for this phase. The administrator starts the server as described in Vicon Consortium [2011b] for interface purpose. The designer starts Siemens NX and creates a virtual prototype in the virtual environment. Figure 4.10 presents the selection of an internal special toolset role in Siemens NX, provided by the installation program having the possibility to start the CAD module from the internal Siemens NX toolbar.

In four steps recommendations are achieved for a design:

1. Create CAD prototypes:
   As seen in the Use Case Diagram (see figure 4.9), the user needs to have an existing object (e.g. press button as cube) in the virtual environment for annotation by the module. Figure 4.11 presents the title screen of Siemens NX including an imported CAD model.

2. Start the CAD module:
   To start the CAD module, a shortcut button was included into Siemens NX (see the small V Icon in the upper corner of figure 4.11). After start, the annotation view is presented.

3. Annotate CAD objects:
   Designers are able to add semantic information about CAD objects using the Annotation View of the CAD module. Figure 4.12 presents the annotation of a CAD object as a press button.

Figure 4.10: Special Vicon Role selection in Siemens NX

4. Get textual recommendation and / or apply recommendation:

Based on semantic information about the annotated objects, qualitative recommendations can be applied to an object immediately. Figure 4.13 presents the recommendation view of the CAD module with the "*Apply Recommendation*" Button.

Designers receive as output all recommendations from the first phase (by VSF import) and component related recommendations annotated to the virtual components. Latter instances can have the relation to different component parameters, e.g. specific attributes of the component including nominal values (e.g. size of a component). For the application of qualitative recommendations, these parameters must be pre-

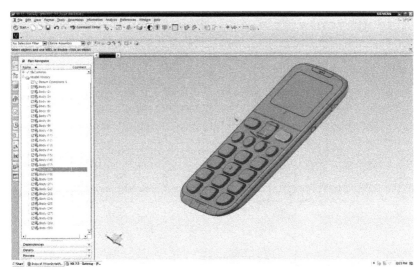

Figure 4.11: Example of a loaded CAD file - DORO mobile phone

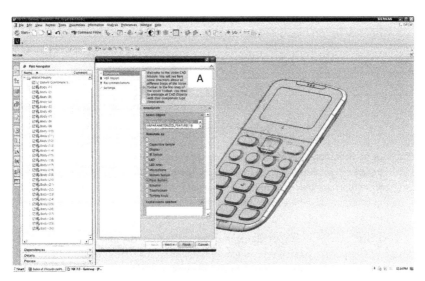

Figure 4.12: Annotation of a CAD object as a press button

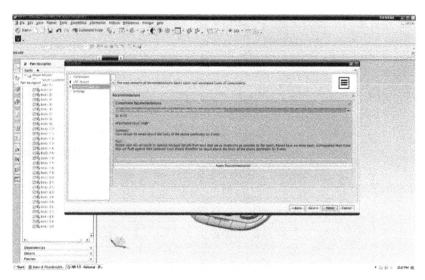

Figure 4.13: Recommendation view in CAD Module

defined by designers (Tools → Expression or Ctrl+E in Siemens NX). The interface presents all relevant parameters during annotation of objects. For example, if one recommendation defines that the button height should be at least 5 mm, the affected parameter name is presented during annotation and must be defined by designers in Siemens NX.

## 4.3 Impact on the Product Development Process

Chapter 2.4 described various customer involvement methods used in different scenarios of product development. Referring to different levels of customer involvement (in terms of this thesis, customers are beneficiaries), the reviewed methods presented three levels: *design for*, *design with* and *design by*. *Design for* describes the perspective of product development to create a product *for* a specified target group, without participation of real persons, representing the target group. Here, designers create the product and decide about changes all by themselves. In *design with* representatives of the target group participate in the design process e.g. within evaluation, but the designer is still creating the product. *Design by* moves this responsibility to the target group entirely.

The method, as presented in this thesis, refers to the inclusion of guidelines into the design process without the involvement of real customers (beneficiaries) into the product development process. The involvement of the target group is handled by context information based on user studies. Also a specification for only one target group or a combination of different groups is possible.

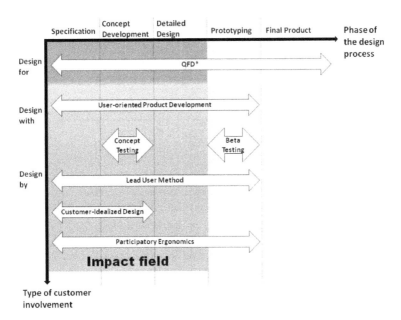

Figure 4.14: Impact on different methods of involvement

Figure 4.14 describes all previously mentioned methods of end user involvement in relation to product development phases. The impact field represents affected phases of the product development process. Referring to the theses of this work (see section 1.6), it is aimed to include the presented tools into product development process phases without an obstruction to the designer. In the first phase (draft) the user is able to use a stand alone system to get recommendations for the desired target group and product type. These textual suggestions for the design process refer to different aspects of the product which are already specified during drafting. For instance if the product should be for visual impaired people, the designer should be aware of large fonts as soon as possible in the product development process. Some recommendations which should be considered, do have a very strong geometrical form and surface impact so already in this phase the designer must be aware of different aspects of the end users.

The second tool can be used within daily-work software of designers as an integrated module of the CAD software Siemens NX. This results in acceptance by the users getting qualitative, but also quantitative recommendations directly applied to product parameters.

All tools create a user awareness with the designers for a proper understanding of impaired user's needs. Product development is no longer an encapsulated process (see 2.1) in which not only the surface of a product and its functional design aspects are considered but also context of the focus group, typical environments, tasks and component specifications. The method provides user involvement by using existing user studies with specified target groups. Also the context information is used through the complete product development process to support designers in the sketch design and CAD phase.

Referring to section 2.4, the software framework can be seen as an **extension to Quality Function Deployment** by an iterative factor. In addition to QFD in each phase the scenario is specified and used to generate quality function similar recommendations based upon predefined specifications.

## 4.4 Conclusion

Based on the implementation of the knowledge base in the previous chapter 3, this chapter presents the implementation of the framework providing a support for designers by providing recommendations based on a pre-specified set of target User Models, typical environments and typical tasks which can be performed using the product.

A system architecture including designer front ends was presented and tools implemented for the purpose of a phase based supporting framework providing designers with qualitative and quantitative recommendations as seen in chapter 3.3.6.

**Hypothesis 2 (*Suitable Reasoning*)**

*Ontology based models can be used to give statements from knowledge base for specified scenarios described by the questions of **who** is using a product **where** to perform **what** task.*

The result presents the answer to hypothesis 2 as a standalone tool presenting qualitative recommendations for sketch design phase and an integrated module in a CAD environment (Siemens NX), which can also apply recommendations directly to existing virtual objects. A server provides recommendations based on ontology based models and reasoning as seen in chapter 3.

With respect to section 2.4, the framework can be seen as an extension to Quality Function Deployment by an iterative factor allowing designers to modify product designs based upon predefined scenario specifications.

Chapter 5 will evaluate the presented framework by the impact on the product development process with involvement of designers and beneficiaries.

# Chapter 5

# Evaluation

This chapter concerns the third hypothesis of chapter 1.6. For a reasonable and comprehensible evaluation, this hypothesis was split into three sub-hypotheses. The first sub-hypothesis concentrates on the account of the general concept of the framework and includes interviews with designers. The second focuses upon the improvement for the complete development process and was implemented including an online questionnaire with end users of the framework and the third targets end users of the products (customer satisfaction), so *real* products were tested with beneficiaries. While section 5.1 concerns the theoretical concept of the system, section 5.2 focuses on the use of the software by designers. Section 5.3 concentrates on the view by real people of the target group directly to see if the products can be used by a wider group of people.

## 5.1 General Concept

### 5.1.1 Thesis and Prediction

**Hypothesis 3.1 (*General Concept*)**

> The concept of supporting designers during product development as a software framework is able to support the design of inclusive products.

For this hypothesis, designers were interviewed. Some designers were without any pre-knowledge others had strong knowledge about ergonomic issues and requirements of elderly people, the software usage and impact on product development process. The aim of these interviews was to get a better understanding of possibilities but also limitations from the designer's perspective.

## 5.1.2 Experimental Setup

The user study is documented in detail in deliverable 4.3 of the VICON project (see Vicon Consortium [2013a]). Four different statements were presented to participants that were already familiar with the software.

## 5.1.3 Execution

### Methodology

As this user study was part of the VICON project, it includes the software package VIRTEX for evaluation of already existing virtual products (see section 2.6.4). The result from this simulation presents different issues and recommendations as in the sketch design and CAD design phases[1].

Statements as listed below were presented to participants asking for agreement. Suggestions of improvements were collected with open questions.

The original study had nine participants, four of them only using the evaluation software tool VIRTEX not part of this thesis. For each statement a Likert (see Likert [1932]) scale with 7 values was presented.

### Statements

The following statements were presented:

1. "The VICON virtual user concept is capable in supporting the designers in creating inclusive products."
   This statement focuses on the complete concept of the VICON project including the framework part, as described by this thesis, but also an evaluation software part VIRTEX for simulation of virtual products is sufficient to create products for a wider group of customers.

2. "The VICON virtual user concept can help to involve the user's perspective into the development process earlier."
   This aims especially the product development phases presented by this thesis to enhance and improve contextual information into the process of design in which designers are creating the product by sketch and the CAD software.

3. "The VICON virtual user concept is capable in product development acceleration."
   Regarding all parts of the software framework, design and evaluation parts should support designers in terms of time which also results in cost decreases of product development.

---

[1] See [Vicon Consortium, 2012b] of the VICON project for more information about VIRTEX

4. "The VICON virtual user concept provides knowledge concerning disabilities and derived requirements."
As a final statement but also for future purposes of the software in terms of learning of contextual information by designers about end customers, this statement aims the purpose to raise the question of user needs by designers to their product.

## 5.1.4 Results

| Statement | ~ | - | +/- | + | ++ | +++ |
|---|---|---|---|---|---|---|
| "The VICON virtual user concept is capable in supporting the designers in creating inclusive products." | 1 | 0 | 0 | 1 | 3 | 0 |
| "The VICON virtual user concept can help to involve the user's perspective into the development process earlier." | 0 | 1 | 1 | 1 | 2 | 0 |
| "The VICON virtual user concept is capable in product development acceleration." | 1 | 1 | 0 | 0 | 2 | 1 |
| "The VICON virtual user concept provides knowledge concerning disabilities and derived requirements." | 0 | 0 | 1 | 0 | 2 | 2 |

Table 5.1: Results of statements about general concept

Table 5.1 presents the results of this user study. The first statement shows the response of participants if the concept is capable of supporting designers in creating inclusive products. All except one participant agreed. The one participant strongly disagreed concerning a complete replacement of user trials with prototypes with the framework. The concept itself may be not capable to replace user tests completely but is able to help and support especially for designers with minor experience in inclusive design guidelines.

**Comments to statement: "The VICON virtual user concept is capable in supporting the designers in creating inclusive products."**

- "It will give a very good reminder to work on inclusive design. After all, you have all the documents, you have no knowledge of. Also if the designer is well knowledgeable, he/she can forget! (S: The system would remind him/her on inclusive design challenges.) For designers with no experience it will be even bigger help."

- "Yes, if it could give more physical data for mechanical engineers."

- "If the model has a sufficient amount of parameters, then yes. I.e. all parameters you need to depict disabilities."

- "It's a tool that can help. But the designer should not trust the software in any case. Otherwise you'll get for ten years always the same stuff. I think inclusive products have to be innovative. And for innovation you need freedom. The database is limiting. Using VICON only as a support of the design process can work, but relying only on the VICON environment can be limiting."

- "You could support but only to a very limited amount. We believe that you need to meet the real users, and you cannot do that in a machine environment."

Regarding the second statement, the answers were diverse. Some participants agreed the concept can help to involve user's perspective into development process earlier, but also considered the issue, that a complete replacement of user trials is not advantageous. Another participant noted that designers should not solely rely on the virtual concept but rather see the system as a supporting tool set than a replacement of user trials.

**Comments to statement: "The VICON virtual user concept can help to involve the user's perspective into the development process earlier."**

- "I'm more hesitant for this statement. The problem is, that the model is put rather late. So that is maybe too late, or for some parts of the design maybe too late. Labelling and textures can still be adapted, but in order to change some forms there are not enough time and money usually available. "

- "This is my opinion for this version of VICON. If VICON is developed and included my opinions above it will be strongly agree"

- "The focus is not on the time, but on the complex information context, which I as a designer get. Things I have to consider are good packed, it's good platform where I could inform myself and get an overview, also before starting the design."

- "Yes, it can, but a good designer should always think about the user's perspective first, before beginning sketching. The question is: Is the data from the database really the user's perspective?"

- "This shouldn't solely rely on the virtual concept, instead of going to the real people. Inclusive design is not a group of people; you cannot summarize all the individuals! Of course there are Personas and categories, but everyone is different."

- "The sketch tool could have some help, it provides a list with recommendations. But we already have it."

One answer to the third statement is interesting in particular. The statement issued, that the system is capable in product development acceleration, but one participant mentioned that it may even result in a deceleration of product development as designers adapt prototypes to user needs. All in all this leads to better products, which is the main issue of the framework.

**Comments to statement: "The VICON virtual user concept is capable in product development acceleration."**

- "No, I don't think so. (S: Thinking on evaluation. However also after I told about Sketch Application the opinion still remained that the acceleration cannot be reached.) It may result even in deceleration. But this is not very negative. It will make better products and that's great! It will make better products, but it will not make it faster. It's a matter of redoing things. (S: It can lead sometimes to redoing things.)"

- "I could imagine that it would accelerate. It depends on the realisation."

- "You can prevent big faults and big mistakes. You can save money and time by virtual prototyping."

- "I think it's really good."

- "If it does, it would probably accelerate in the wrong direction. So we'll get not so good products, very fast. If you find a way to make it more accurate, some products could be helped, if they are easier to map. The mobile phones are more complex than the tool currently can handle. Currently the tool is oversimplifying the reality. There might be products, where it could help, but for mobile phones it is too simple."

The last statement issues the aim of the framework to provide knowledge concerning disabilities and derived requirements, which except one participant agreed. One participant neither agreed or disagreed and stated that the system provides useful knowledge but it needs sophisticated data about the end users such as a high amount of recommendations.

**Comments to statement: "The VICON virtual user concept provides knowledge concerning disabilities and derived requirements."**

- "Yes, it's what it is about."

- "It provides me with this knowledge."

- "You learn a lot about humans with disabilities. The text is always about humans and devices."

- "Well, there was some really good knowledge. The list from the sketch tool is useful, but if you base test on the too limited data, it could mislead the designers in their process."

**Further suggestions for improvement**

- "Usage of VICON in any CAD software; 1. VICON could give us physical data (dimensions, colours, if needs light and sound, forces, ...) 2. This data must be given to the engineers during design (interactive) on time.

- "I missed an active part of designing! E.g. if I would be designing a mobile phone, I would like to combine the designing part in the CAD program and directly get a visual feedback notifying me about some problems."

- "Sometimes there is no target user group specified, so it would be helpful to have a possibility to adjust the parameters of the users, environments etc. i.e. to create your own profiles."

- "The CAD application had a lot of problems installing it. I wish the application would be more available to different platforms. OS X version would be also great! But, thank you to your work, it was an eye opener!"

- "Whenever there is risk that the information can be misguided, it is best to highlight it well. The tools are not able to replace the real user tests. But if you say, this is something that should point out the issues of a product that need to be tested with real users, then the tool can be really useful"

### 5.1.5 Discussion

In summary, this evaluation issued that the concept of the system including an evaluation software for virtual prototypes does have a good basis but the amount of information needs to improve. In the next section designers using the software in their product development review the system more specifically. Regarding the answers of the participants, three main issues were identified:

- The system is as useful as data and recommendations provided.

- With the system it is possible to prevent big faults and big mistakes before prototyping.

- It does not necessarily lead to an acceleration, but can also result in a deceleration due to product customization to user needs.

## 5.2 Improvement for Development Process

This section is an expert evaluation with designers to obtain a value of acceptance, suitability and usability of the software framework in product development environments.

An online questionnaire was done based on ISO-9241-110 (Schneider [2008]) with focus on usability and end-user suitability of the software framework.

### 5.2.1 Thesis and Prediction

In this section the following hypothesis will be concerned.

**Hypothesis 3.2 (*Improvement for Development Process*)**

> *The software framework is suitable to be adapted into existing product development processes and can be used by designers without hindrance to their typical tasks.*

The main question of hypothesis 3.1 deals with the manipulations of current product development processes by the system. To analyse the change, a questionnaire was created in which designers actively use the system. It is based upon the ISO-9241-110 (Schneider [2008]).

The result of this evaluation refers to designer acceptance directly, but is also connected to user involvement methods applied by design studios. It is a crucial issue for designers to use the presented tools without hindrance. As seen in section 2.4, there is a variety of methods available to involve customers in product development. The independent integration of applied user involvement methods during product development is crucial for a successful acceptance by designers, so an optimal result would be positive regardless of the method applied by participants of the study.

## 5.2.2 Experimental Setup

The framework consists of two different end-user applications, as explained in chapter 4. Both applications can be used after the installation using a software installer implemented using a scriptable install system[1]. During the online questionnaire, the installer can be downloaded and used to set up the Sketch Design Tool (4.2.1) and the Siemens NX module, which is installed automatically if a local installation of Siemens NX is available.

In the current version, only Windows OS is supported[2]. The evaluation itself was implemented using HTML[3] and PHP[4] to create a questionnaire capable of providing an installer during the process but also raising the questions.

## 5.2.3 Execution

### Methodology

The aim of this evaluation is to obtain a value for designer acceptance and the impact on existing product development processes. As target participants 11 physical product designers were interviewed.

The first questions referred to the familiarity of participants with inclusive design and Virtual User Models.

Figure 3 presents a bar graph of participant knowledge about inclusive design. Most participants are partners of the VICON project so they were already familiar. Virtual User Model (see 3.3) contain contextual information about target end users of products. VUMs were more often discussed and reviewed during the project process than inclusive design in general, so participants were more familiar with this term (see figure 4).

---

[1]NSIS (Nullsoft Scriptable Install System) is a professional open source system to create Windows installers. It is designed to be as small and flexible as possible and is therefore very suitable for the presented framework. See http://nsis.sourceforge.net/

[2]The questionnaire can be executed using a browser and the address: http://134.102.95.211/eval.

[3]See http://www.w3.org/html/

[4]See http://php.net/

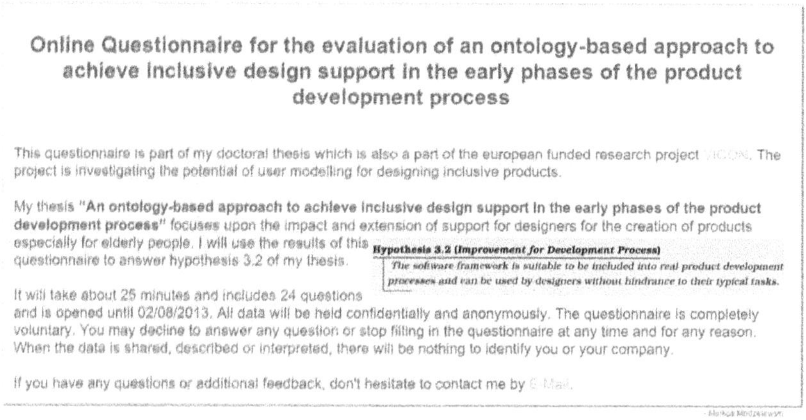

Online Questionnaire for the evaluation of an ontology-based approach to achieve inclusive design support in the early phases of the product development process

This questionnaire is part of my doctoral thesis which is also a part of the european funded research project ....... The project is investigating the potential of user modelling for designing inclusive products.

My thesis "An ontology-based approach to achieve inclusive design support in the early phases of the product development process" focuses upon the impact and extension of support for designers for the creation of products especially for elderly people. I will use the results of this questionnaire to answer hypothesis 3.2 of my thesis.

**Hypothesis 3.2 (Improvement for Development Process)**
The software framework is suitable to be included into real product development processes and can be used by designers without hindrance to their typical tasks.

It will take about 25 minutes and includes 24 questions and is opened until 02/08/2013. All data will be held confidentially and anonymously. The questionnaire is completely voluntary. You may decline to answer any question or stop filling in the questionnaire at any time and for any reason. When the data is shared, described or interpreted, there will be nothing to identify you or your company.

If you have any questions or additional feedback, don't hesitate to contact me by E-Mail.

Figure 5.1: Introduction of questionnaire

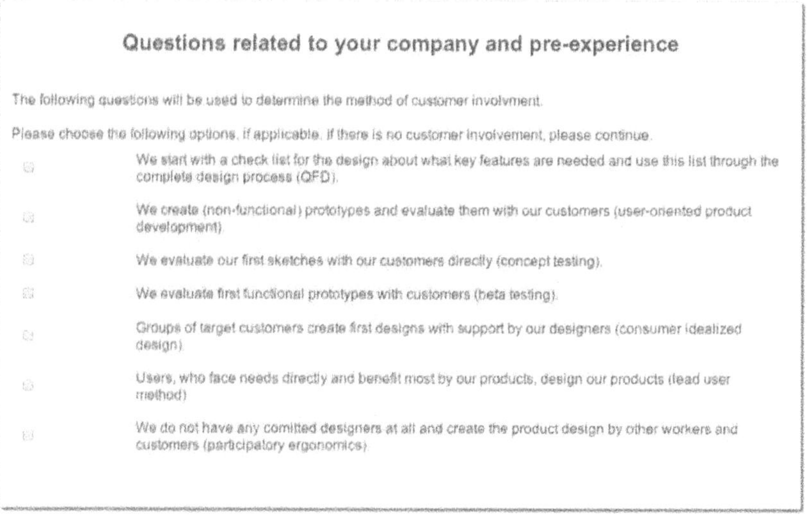

Questions related to your company and pre-experience

The following questions will be used to determine the method of customer involvment.

Please choose the following options, if applicable. If there is no customer involvement, please continue.

- We start with a check list for the design about what key features are needed and use this list through the complete design process (QFD).
- We create (non-functional) prototypes and evaluate them with our customers (user-oriented product development).
- We evaluate our first sketches with our customers directly (concept testing).
- We evaluate first functional prototypes with customers (beta testing).
- Groups of target customers create first designs with support by our designers (consumer idealized design).
- Users, who face needs directly and benefit most by our products, design our products (lead user method).
- We do not have any comitted designers at all and create the product design by other workers and customers (participatory ergonomics).

Figure 5.2: Questions related to customer involvement method

The online questionnaire starts with general information about the topic and the aim of this study. The first questions relate to personal information including pre knowledge about inclusive design and Virtual User Modelling for later classification. In addition and as presented in section 2.4, the type of customer involvement is asked (see figure 5.2).

In the next step participants used the installer mentioned above. The questionnaire is seen divided into 2 different parts. The first part deals with the explanation of both tools (sketch design tool and cad module) including questions related to the use and complexity. The second part contains questions related to ISO Norm 9241-110 (see Schneider [2008]).

The sketch design tool is described by an explanation of all input fields for designers as presented in figure 5.3:

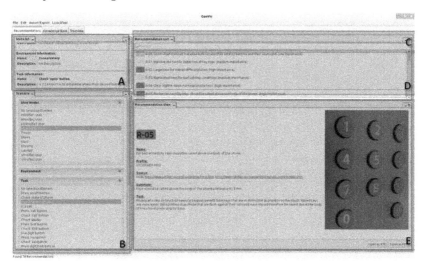

Figure 5.3: Mainframe explanation of the sketch design tool during the online questionnaire

There is section (A) Meta Information about the current scenario selection is seen. Also impairment levels for each user model instance are presented in this field: HProfile1 = mild hearing impaired, HProfile2 = moderate hearing impaired, VProfile for visual and MDProfile for manual dexterity impaired User Model.

In section (B) designers can select user model representatives (Personas), typical environments in which the target product can be used and typical tasks which can be performed using the product. A multiselection is also possible.

A search field is presented in section (C), in which designers can search for recommendations (e.g. the search term "button" will result in a recommendation list with only relevant button recommendations).

Section (D) presents a list including all resulting recommendations based on the current selection of User Model, Environment and Task or search.

The full text of one single recommendation is presented in section (E). It includes a name, required impairment profiles, source, summary and a text containing relevant information.

For the test, a use case scenario is described. The participant has to imagine designing a product for a fictional end user called Eileen where the Persona Eileen is described as followed:

> Eileen retired a few years ago, at the same time as her husband. She has mild/moderate hearing and manual dexterity impairments, but they don't affect her everyday life. She does not wear a hearing aid but is aware that she is listening to the TV much louder these days and would probably benefit from a hearing aid. She has no visual loss, so does not wear glasses or contact lenses.
> Eileen is generally healthy and active. In the week she helps look after her young grandchildren and at weekends she enjoys travelling and gardening with her husband.

This scenario also raises the issue to the participants, "How do you know what is important for the design, if you do not have any experience with products for impaired people?". The sketch design tool can be used to get design support for this exact situation, based upon different guidelines as already mentioned (see 3.3.6).

**Questionnaire**

After the presentation of inclusive design issue and each software front end, questions are raised.

The questions relate to ISO Norm 9241-110 (see Schneider [2008]) with four categories according to the following themes:

- Suitability for the task
  Does the software help designers to complete a task of product design for elderly people without burden?

- Self-descriptiveness
  Each software tool explained sufficiently and comprehensive?

- Conformity with the expectations
  Is the structure of the software ok and does it conform with habits of designers?

- Suitability for learning
  Do the tools require pre knowledge?

## 5.2.4  Results

| Personal knowledge of participants about ... | not at all familiar | slightly familiar | moderately familiar | familiar | very familiar |
|---|---|---|---|---|---|
| ...Design of physical products | 0 | 3 | 0 | 1 | 7 |
| ...Computer-Aided Design | 0 | 3 | 1 | 3 | 4 |
| ...Inclusive Design | 0 | 1 | 3 | 6 | 1 |
| ...Virtual User Modelling (VUM) | 0 | 5 | 2 | 4 | 0 |

Table 5.2: Results of questions regarding personal knowledge of participants

### General Questions

Table 5.2 presents the results of the general questions about pre knowledge of each participant. 8 participants describe themselves as familiar or very familiar about design of physical products (8 / 11 ~ 72%). As mentioned in 5.2.3, mostly designers were questioned but also three researchers in the field of design participated[1]. The reason was to get a more resourceful perspective on the results from practical but also theoretical point of view on design and ergonomic factors.

The answers of CAD knowledge are due to the fact not all designers work with a virtual environment but rather with sketch drafts or other tools. All participants are at least slightly familiar with CAD. Both front ends were evaluated by each experience level of designers.
Although not all participants were experienced in CAD, a strong familiarity with inclusive design was there.
All participants were at least slightly familiar with Virtual User Models. The group of participants of this evaluation is thus appropriate.

All described methods of customer involvement were applied:

- Quality function deployment (QFD) 7/11[2]

- User-oriented product development 1/11

- Concept testing 3/11

- Beta testing 3/11

- Consumer idealized design 1/11

- Lead user method 3/11

- Participatory ergonomics 1/11

As expected, QFD is the most used method (see also section 2.4 or Akao [2004]). The group of participants is suitable as the modification of the product development process does have a strong impact on this method (see section 4.3). Both Concept testing and beta testing were used by the same amount, one participant described both together. Lead user method, concept and beta testing were applied in combination with QFD, as they do not cover the complete product development process.

---

[1]Answers only differ in applied customer involvement methods as researchers selected none.
[2]3/11 participants from research selected none applied customer involvement method.

The coverage of involvement methods is positive with respect to the inclusion of the software framework into different product development processes. Each method was applied by at least one participant of this study.

**Suitability for the task**

| Statement | - - | - | +/- | + | ++ | skip |
|---|---|---|---|---|---|---|
| "The Sketch Application provides a wide choice of scenarios." | 0 | 2 | 5 | 2 | 2 | 0 |
| "The design recommendations of the toolset are necessary." | 0 | 0 | 0 | 5 | 6 | 0 |
| "It takes a short time to go through recommendation list." | 2 | 1 | 3 | 3 | 2 | 0 |
| "I would need a user manual to use the software." | 0 | 1 | 3 | 6 | 1 | 0 |
| "The look and feel of the application was suitable and pleasant." | 0 | 2 | 3 | 4 | 2 | 0 |
| "The software is easy to use." | 0 | 2 | 0 | 8 | 0 | 1 |

Table 5.3: Results of questions regarding suitability for the task

The suitability of the software framework to be added into existing product development processes is covered in this section. Table 5.3 presents these results.

The first statement is questioning if the choice of scenarios of user model, typical environment in which the product would be used and typical task performed using the product is sufficient enough. The result is slightly positive but ambiguous. Almost half of participants answered neutrally (5/11 answered "+/-"), infers that the current system describes a good base but can (and probably should) also be extended.

The necessity of design recommendations is throughout answered very positive. All participants agreed, resulting in the conclusion that the concept of a recommendation-driven product development process is not just accepted but also needed. Although the customer involvement method applied by each participant is very different, the inclusion of recommendations is advantageous independently of involvement method applied.

The variety of approval about the time consumption to go through the recommendation list can be seen very ambiguous (see figure 7). While on the one side it would be time and cost saving to be able to go through the recommendations very fast, on the other side a deceleration of product design would be more fruitful with respect to more accessible products and designer creativity. The aim of this question was to maintain this assumption. This will also be an issue in the next section of the evaluation.

The next two statements were answered very similarly with a trend to approval (figure 8 and 9). Participants of the study would need a user manual to the software and the look and feel of the software was suitable and pleasant. Regarding the front end presentation, the results are slightly positive but can also be improved.

The last question of this section described the approval to the general statement that the software is easy to use. Eight participants approved this ("+" bar in table 5.3), while 2 disapproved ("-") and one skipped this question. The strong approval concludes that the software in its current state is already easy to use by designers but can be improved. One participant could not use the software directly on the own pc and commented that he was not able to install and use the software on a Mac OS.

**Self-Descriptiveness**

| Statement | - - | - | +/- | + | ++ | skip |
|---|---|---|---|---|---|---|
| "The description of information in the sketch application for user profiles is comprehensible." | 0 | 1 | 1 | 6 | 3 | 0 |
| "The description of information in the sketch application for environments is comprehensible." | 0 | 1 | 1 | 4 | 3 | 2 |
| "The description of information in the sketch application for tasks is comprehensible." | 0 | 1 | 1 | 7 | 2 | 0 |
| "The description about recommendations is comprehensible." | 0 | 1 | 0 | 7 | 3 | 0 |

Table 5.4: Results of questions regarding self-descriptiveness

Information on user profiles, environments, tasks and recommendations is collected next (see table 5.4). The results show a trend towards approval (most participants answered "+"), concluding a general approval but also some ambiguities with respect to comprehension of each model. More information about the scenario would be advantageous. As presented in figure 5.3 part (A), meta information about the current scenario selection can be seen in the software. For instance impairment levels for each user model instance are presented, but designers do not exactly understand the meaning. An improvement of the scenario explanation would be beneficial.

**Conformity with user expectations**

| Statement | - - | - | +/- | + | ++ | skip |
|---|---|---|---|---|---|---|
| "The software has a consistent structure." | 0 | 0 | 3 | 7 | 1 | 0 |
| "The layout was as expected." | 0 | 1 | 2 | 6 | 1 | 1 |
| "Some features of applications do not have an unpredictable processing time (e.g. start of application)." | 0 | 0 | 2 | 6 | 0 | 3 |

Table 5.5: Results of questions regarding conformity with user expectations

The structure of the software was mostly approved by participants as seen in table 5.5. The layout was similar to expectations of designers. This leads to the assumption of a positive conformity with user expectations. The last statement, that some features of applications do not have an unpredictable processing time was slightly approved. Some participants skipped this question, because they could not find any features with unpredictable processing time, so they were unclear about the result. Eight participants found some. For instance the start of the application takes some time which is unclear from designers perspective. As previously mentioned in chapter 4, during the start the reasoning is performed from an initial Ontology inferring a new resulting model which is used in the application. In the current state, the model is inferred dynamically by every start of the application regarding further implementations and extensions of the model itself.

**Suitability for learning**

| Statement | - - | - | +/- | + | ++ | skip |
|---|---|---|---|---|---|---|
| "The software requires little time to learn." | 0 | 1 | 5 | 4 | 1 | 0 |
| "The software is easy to learn without prior knowledge, help or manual." | 1 | 1 | 2 | 7 | 0 | 0 |
| "The software is easy to use, even without having prior knowledge." | 0 | 3 | 2 | 6 | 0 | 0 |

Table 5.6: Results of questions regarding conformity with user expectations

The first statement asks how time consuming it is to learn how to use the software (see table 5.6). In average the result of this statement was slightly positive among participants, concluding that it takes some time to learn. The next both statements consolidate this statement, regarding the software is easy to learn without prior knowledge, help or manual with a strong agree by participants. This goes in line with the conclusion of results that a user manual would be advantageous.

## 5.2.5   Discussion

The evaluation of the software framework by designers showed that user involvement methods applied by design studios of participants vary, the assumption can be made that the software can be included independently of the current used method. In conclusion, two main issues were identified:

- The software is suitable to be included in existing product development processes independently of user involvement method applied.
  This issue is the main result of this part of the evaluation. All 7 customer involvement methods were covered by participants but also each participant stated a positive feedback. Especially results about the necessity of design recommendations (see second question of table 5.3 or figure 6 of the annex) emphasized the need by designers for a recommendation-driven product development process.

- An improvement regarding more comprehensive scenario information is advantageous.
  Designers do not fully comprehend the scenario of their selection and how it is processed. A further development as a user manual including background information or an extension of meta information would allow a more sophisticated scenario selection by designers.

## 5.3 Customer Satisfaction

### 5.3.1 Thesis and Prediction

**Hypothesis 3.3 (*Customer Satisfaction*)**

*End products, which are created using the framework, can be used by a wider range of customers.*

This hypothesis was evaluated with end-customers (beneficiaries) of the products, which are elderly and impaired people. With respect to the framework, this evaluation mostly deals with content and output of the system itself but not functionality. Different products were evaluated which were created with and withouth the framework to review the discrepancy between answers of beneficiaries. Tests with products and mild to moderate impaired people were conducted, in which participants evaluated end design issues by themselves.

Products, which were created without the framework, should result in more problematic issues by the end users than products created with the framework. As an optimal result, products created using the framework would have no accessibility issues at all.

In addition to user trials, an expert evaluation by an accessibility expert of NCBI was conducted as part of the VICON project. Results are divided into general comments and a checklist evaluation with respect to recommendations produced by the system. The expert evaluation was carried out with the devices Doro Mock-Up Phone (see table 5.9), Washing Machine Panel 1 and 2 (see table 5.11).

### 5.3.2 Experimental Setup

The study took place in Ireland and Germany (see Focus Group Report of the VICON project Vicon Consortium [2013b]). A total of 48 subjects participated, all over the age of 65[1]. All participants had at least one mild to moderate hearing, vision or manual dexterity impairment (appendix 6.2 presents the full list of participants).

Concerning the individual impairments table 5.8 presents the levels of each impairment type by categories of none, mild and moderate impaired subjects.

As washing machine panels were not available during the beneficiary tests, an additional accessibility expert evaluation as an alternative to the beneficiary testing has been conducted to assess the washing machine panels.

---

[1]One participant has had severe vision impairment, so was excluded from the study

| Age | Male | Female | Total |
|---|---|---|---|
| 65 - 69 years | 5 | 6 | 11 |
| 70 - 79 years | 1 | 9 | 10 |
| 80 - 89 years | 5 | 8 | 13 |
| 90+ years | 0 | 5 | 5 |
| **Total** | 10 | 29 | 39 |

Table 5.7: Participants of the user study by age and gender

| Impairment type | None | Mild | Moderate |
|---|---|---|---|
| Hearing | 19 | 19 | 9 |
| Vision | 7 | 18 | 22 |
| Manual Dexterity | 27 | 14 | 6 |

Table 5.8: Participants of the user study by impairment levels

### 5.3.3 Execution

**Methodology**

According to the hypothesis, this evaluation focuses upon end users of customer products. A study with people over 65 years of age who have mild to moderate hearing, vision and/or manual dexterity impairments was executed, in which the participants should access different products and perform predefined tasks. Two different categories of products were evaluated:

1. Existing User Interfaces

   This category involves the evaluation of different products without the use and application of the framework. Resulting issues should be similar to recommendations implemented in the framework.

2. Emerged User Interfaces

   This part of the study focuses upon the use of products, which were created with focus to inclusive design and usability by elderly people. The result is compared to results of the first category.

After both evaluations, issues and problems regarding the usability and accessibility were collected using interviews with participants.

**Examined Products**

Regarding existing user interfaces, the following tables 5.9, 5.10 and 5.11 present the used products[1].

Both industrial partners of the VICON project provided emerged products with focus

---

[1]Larger images in appendix 6.2

to issues of elderly customers. Regarding washing machine panels, Arçelik panel 1 was created for inclusive design purposes but without the use of the framework.

Due to the fact, that the emerged user interfaces are prototypes at an early stage, and do not have the full functionality as existing user interfaces, it was not possible to perform tasks as receive a call or send a text message when using the mock-up (table 5.9).

**Executed Tasks**

With respect to product functionality, different tasks were performed by participants of the study. Some tasks on the mobile phone mock-up could not be performed due to non-functionality of prototypes.

*Mobile Phones (figure 5.9)*

- Identify "on" button
  In the Doro PhoneEasy®332 the "on" button is the same as the "off" button. It is visible as a small IEC 5010 power symbol on the red disconnect call button. In the Mock-Up phone, this button (as all buttons) is the same, but without the power symbol.

- Successfully dial a number
  The participants should dial a number and tell if any problems occurred.

- Press "green" button to connect call
  The "green" button is marked as a telephone handset and placed similarly on both phones. On the Mock-Up Phone all button labels were white.

- Identify that a call is coming in
  This task could not be evaluated with the Mock-Up Phone due to non-functionality.

- Press "green" button to receive call
  This task could not be evaluated with the Mock-Up Phone due to non-functionality.

- Identify the "message" button (SMS)
  On the 332, the button presents the letters "SMS". On the Mock-Up the button is represented as an envelope also on the right side.

- Open and read an incoming text message
  On both mobile phones, participants had to press the "message" button to open and read an incoming text message.

| Source - Model | Physical Characteristics | Image |
|---|---|---|
| Doro - Doro PhoneEasy ® 332 | • Small IEC 5010 power symbol on red button for "on" and "off" over a telephone handset.<br><br>• Receive call button marked green with telephone handset.<br><br>• "SMS" button for messaging.<br><br>• Width: 102mm, length: 50mm, height: 16mm. | |
| Doro - Doro Mock-Up created using the framework | • High button spacing.<br><br>• All buttons labels are white.<br><br>• "On" and "off" button similar to PhoneEasy®332 but without IEC 5010 power symbol.<br><br>• Messaging button marked with an envelope.<br><br>• Width: 123mm, length: 53mm, height: 16mm. | |

Table 5.9: Existing and emerged mobile phones used for evaluation of customer satisfaction

| Source - Model | Physical Characteristics | Image |
|---|---|---|
| Arçelik - Grundig large silver | • IEC 5010 power symbol<br>• Volume Up/Down on lower left as a right triangle marked with "+" and "-".<br>• Channel Up/Down on lower right as "P" with "+" and "-".<br>• Width: 50mm, length: 224mm, height: 12mm at lowest, 22mm at highest point, height increases gradually from top to bottom. | |
| Arçelik - Grundig large black | • IEC 5010 power symbol<br>• Volume Up/Down on lower left marked with "-" and "+" on the left and right outer circle in the middle.<br>• Channel Up/Down on lower right as "P+" and "P-" on the top and bottom outer circle in the middle.<br>• Width: 45mm, length: 240mm, height: 17mm. | |
| Arçelik - Grundig small black | • IEC 5010 power symbol<br>• Volume Up/Down on lower left marked with "-" and "+" on the left and right outer circle in the middle.<br>• Channel Up/Down on lower right as "^" and "-" on the top and bottom outer circle in the middle.<br>• Width: 50mm, length: 110mm, height: 17mm at lowest, 27mm at highest point, height increases gradually from top to bottom. | |

Table 5.10: Existing and emerged remote controls used for evaluation of customer satisfaction

117

| Source - Model | Physical Characteristics | Image |
|---|---|---|
| Arçelik - Arçelik Washing Machine Panel 1 | • "On / Off" button on the right side of the panel with a IEC 5010 power symbol.<br>• Program selection as rotary knob in the middle with 12 settings.<br>• Buttons and rotary knob are grey coloured.<br>• Different labelling (e.g. under hand symbol "Start / Pause / Cancel" button).<br>• LED information panel between program knob and detergent dispenser.<br>• Width: 590mm, height 125mm at shortest point and 150mm at longest point. | |
| Arçelik - Arçelik Washing Machine Panel 2 | • "On / Off" button on the right side of the panel with a IEC 5010 power symbol.<br>• Only colored button is "Start / Pause / Cancel" button.<br>• Program selection as rotary knob in the middle with 16 settings.<br>• LED information panel between program knob and detergent dispenser.<br>• "+" and "-" buttons with small gap between them.<br>• Width: 590mm, height 125mm at shortest point and 150mm at longest point. | |

Table 5.11: Existing and emerged washing machines used for evaluation of customer satisfaction

*TV Remotes (figure 5.10)*

- Identify "on" button
  Typically the "on" button on TV Remotes is presented as a red or red-labelled IEC 5010 power symbol. On all evaluated TV Remotes it is placed similarly on the top right of the remote.

- Press "on" button
  Participants were asked in this task to press the identified button.

- Identify the "volume" button
  On the Grundig large silver remote control, the volume buttons are located on the lower half of the remote on the left side, presented including a triangle. On both other remote controls, "+" and "-" buttons are used.

- Press Volume up/down key
  The Grundig large silver has top-bottom alignment of the buttons. Both other devices a left-right alignment.

- Identify the "channel up" button
  On all remote controls, this button is located nearby the volume buttons.

- Press the "channel up" button
  The "channel up" button is located on the lower half of the Grundig silver large remote control. On the Grundig black large it is realized as the "P+" in the middle and on the Grundig small black as "∧".

- Identify location of compartment to change batteries
  On all remote controls, the location of compartment is on the lower back side of the device.

- Identify how to open battery compartment
  This task aims to describe problems with the handling, force and precision needed to open the compartment.

*Washing Machines (figure 5.11)*

- Identify the "on/off" button
  On both washing machine panels the "on/off" button is located on the right side of the panel.

- Push "on/off" button
  This task aims to describe problems with the force and precision needed to push the button.

119

- Identify the set Program
  On both washing machine panels the program setting was realized as a rotary knob in the middle right of the panel.

- Turn knob to set Program
  This task aims to describe problems with the force and precision needed to rotate the knob.

- Identify main control panel
  On both panels the main control panel is located in the lower middle.

- Read and understand texts of main panel
  This task aims to describe problems with labels of the rotary knob.

- Identify minor control panel
  On both panels, the minor control panel is located in the middle.

- Read and understand texts of minor panel
  This task aims to describe problems with labels of the minor panel.

**Product Comparison**

A product comparison was made and separated into three feature categories:

- Cognitive features:
  Potential issues identified in both panels included those relating to the order of use and possible difficulties with interpretation of labels (use of unfamiliar terms and visual formatting to communicate information).

- Sensory features:
  Potential issues included by increasing the labels, the spacing between labels decreased and they became harder to distinguish as well as a lack of audible feedback from the buttons.

- Physical features:
  Potential issues related to the buttons and controls being difficult to press and turn.

## 5.3.4 Results

The following results show the summary of the user trials (complete tables are included in appendix 6.2). An expert evaluation was conducted by an NCBI accessibility expert. The results are divided into general comments (positive and negative) and the results of the checklist evaluation.

### Mobile Phones

In this section results regarding mobile phones are presented. It consists of four parts. General comments (table 5.12) present the expert evaluation by an NCBI accessibility expert. Table 5.13 shows the checklist of recommendation provided by the software framework (also by NCBI accessibility expert). Table 5.14 summarizes the results of the beneficiary study with real participants as mentioned in section 5.3.2. The last table 5.15 presents the result comparison regarding mobile phones.

| Positive | Negative |
|---|---|
| • Button size is good.<br><br>• Numeric labels are clear.<br><br>• Colour contrast is good. | • Space between buttons 1-2-3 is too far apart, causing the phone to be too wide. As a result it would be difficult to hold and use the phone in one hand.<br><br>• There is no obvious on/off button.<br><br>• The function of A, B and C buttons is not obvious.<br><br>• The A, B and C buttons are in a particularly prominent location. It is not clear why they need to be given a prime location, when not every user will use them. It seems they could be easy to accidentally hit off.<br><br>• It is not clear how you would select a menu option on the screen. There is an up-down button in the top centre of the keypad, but there is no OK or select button(s). |

Table 5.12: General Comments - Doro Mock-Up Phone

| Recommendation | Result |
|---|---|
| **Keypad** | |
| Good visual contrast between keys and body of the phone. | Pass |
| Key tops should be convex or flat with a raised edge. | Pass |
| Keys should be as large as possible without reducing the distance between the keys to less than half the key width. | Pass |
| Ideally the keys should be internally illuminated, but the internal illumination should not reduce the legibility of the numbers in daylight. | N/A |
| The visual markings on the keys should be high contrast, clear, and as large as is possible on the key top. | Pass |
| Keys should be raised above the body of the phone (preferably by 5 mm). | Pass |
| The pressure to activate a key should be between 0.5 and 1 Newton. | N/A |
| There should be auditory and tactual feedback of key activation. | N/A |
| Function keys should be tactually discernible from the numeric keys. | Pass |
| There should be a tactual indication on the '5' key or on a QWERTY keyboard on the 'F' and 'J' keys. | Pass |
| A voice mode selection that announces all key presses. | N/A |
| One-touch buttons are provided for ease of calling telephone numbers stored in the memory. | Pass |
| Provide rotational or linear-stop controls. | N/A |
| For keys that do not have any physical travel, audio or tactile feedback should be provided so the user knows when the key has been activated (e.g. a toggle switch or a push-in/pop-out switch). | N/A |
| There is the ability to switch on or off any buttons on the side of the telephone. | Fail |
| Where timed responses are required allow the user to adjust them or set the amount of time allocated to the task. | N/A |
| **Physical Characteristics** | |
| The phone should be easy to hold by someone with a weak grip. | Fail |
| There should not be parts which can easily come off. | Pass |
| The phone should be able to lie on a table and be operated one-handed (non-slip material on the underside of the phone would help to hold the phone in place if it is used while lying on a table). | N/A |
| Any external antenna should be robust and not require extending by the user. | Pass |
| **Result** | **10/12** |

Table 5.13: Recommendation Checklist of Doro Mock-Up Phone

| Task | Doro PhoneEasy®332 | Doro Mock-Up Phone |
|---|---|---|
| Identify "on" button | 20/38 | 7/19 |
| Successfully dial a number | 38/38 | 19/19 |
| Press "green" button to connect call | 37/38 | 18/19 |
| Identify that a call is coming in | 38/38 | N/A |
| Press "green" button to receive call | 38/38 | N/A |
| Identify the "message" button (SMS) | 7/17 | 8/16 |
| Open and read an incoming text message | 25/27 | 16/16 |
| **Total** | 83.4% | N/A |

Table 5.14: Results of user study regarding mobile phones

| Difficulty encountered | Doro PhoneEasy®332 | Doro Mock-Up |
|---|---|---|
| **Cognitive features** | | |
| Difficulty recognizing SMS button | Yes | Yes (but envelope icon was easier than SMS, in Ireland) |
| **Sensory features** | | |
| Difficulty identifying on button | Yes | Yes |
| Difficulty identifying off button | Yes | Yes |
| Difficulty reading letters or numbers | Yes | No |
| **Physical features** | | |
| Difficulty with the size of the buttons (height was too narrow) | Yes | No |
| Difficulty with the spacing of the buttons (too spaced) | No | Yes |
| Difficulty with the spacing of the buttons (not enough space vertically) | Yes | No |
| Difficulty with the shape of the buttons | Yes | No |
| **Total number of issues** | **7** | **4** |

Table 5.15: Result comparison regarding mobile phones

The result of the study of the two mobile phones Doro PhoneEasy®332 and Doro Mock-Up was limited due to non-functionality of the Mock-Up. Cognitive, sensory and physical difficulties of use could be identified (5.15).

The side-by-side comparison suggests that the Mock-Up Phone has less accessibility issues than the existing phone. Especially some physical issues were no longer present in the Mock-Up.

The tests revealed, that for some customers there was not enough vertical spacing between front side buttons of the Doro PhoneEasy®332. On the Mock-Up phone, greater spacing between the buttons resulted in an increased overall size of the phone, so some beneficiaries were unable to use the phone one-handed as desired. This suggests that an optimal spacing between buttons lies somewhere between the 332 and the Mock-up.

There is a direct link between button size, button shape and button spacing. By changing one, it is possible to eliminate problematic issues of others. If buttons are too big and too spaced, the product can be less comfortable to use. To get an appropriate optimal setting, additional beneficiary trials to compare modified interfaces or iterative testing with prototypes is necessary. In the presented user tests, problems with the 332 such as difficulties with the size of the buttons were solved with the Mock-Up. But new problematic issues were created as difficulties with the spacing of the buttons. Similar links can also been found on other interfaces. In the current framework version, the links can only be included as qualitative recommendations. Regarding quantitative recommendations an extension would be needed to include recommendations as functions depending on more than one parameter (which also requires new user trials for the definition of parameters and values).

The use of the envelope logo rather than the term SMS was more in line with inclusive design guidelines, as the term SMS could be classified as technical terminology or country-specific terminology, being unfamiliar in some countries (e.g. Ireland). The choice of a logo instead of text leads to overcome barriers relating to language or literacy.

A quick survey[1] reveals that either one or a combination of three commonly used icons is used: the term "SMS", an envelope or a speech bubble. Also a combination of these is possible, e.g. a "SMS" in a speech bubble. An universal icon for "SMS" is

[1] By looking at ISO and ETSI Standards relating to pictograms, using a Google image search using the terms "text message icon" and "SMS icon". Most commonly used mobile phone operating systems (Android, iOS, Windows Phone) have their own standard icons, but can also be replaced by new themes.

not available.

Also the recent evolution from mobile to smart phones as mentioned in section 1.1 increases the dilemma, since icons are needed that differentiate not just between simple SMS text message, voice mail or email but also different new feature applications such as facebook/google+ messenger, skype chat etc.

One solution implemented by the framework includes internationally recognised standards in icons, pictograms and symbols as recommendations.

This part of the evaluation also covers a comparison of output of the framework with the real prototype design. Recommendation lists provided by the framework were compared with the Doro Mock-Up phone (see 5.13), if the recommendations were applied correctly or not. One issue not included in the Mock-Up relates to holding issue of beneficiaries with a weak grip. Since the material of the Doro Mock-Up phone and so weight and surface material of the functioning phone was not available, results (10 of 12 issues for Doro Mock-Up) shows that recommendations were almost properly applied.

## TV Remotes

In this section results of the TV remote user study with beneficiaries are presented.

| Task | Grundig large silver | Grundig large black | Grundig small black |
|---|---|---|---|
| Identify "on" button | 31/39 | 22/39 | 37/39 |
| Press "on" button | 39/39 | 39/39 | 39/39 |
| Identify the "volume" button | 29/39 | 32/39 | 37/39 |
| Press Volume up/down key | 39/39 | 39/39 | 39/39 |
| Identify the "channel up" button | 38/39 | 35/39 | 24/39 |
| Press the "channel up" button | 39/39 | 39/39 | 39/39 |
| Identify location of compartment to change batteries | 19/20 | 39/39 | 36/38 |
| Identify how to open compartment | 19/20 | 37/38 | 36/38 |
| **Total** | 92.66% | 94.45% | 92.6% |

Table 5.16: Results of user study regarding tv remotes

TV remotes do not have any emerged user interfaces to be compared to, so the results can not be included as a side-by-side comparison. The results of the user trials show only a very small difference in accessibility issues (Grundig large silver: 92.66%, Grundig large black: 94.45%, Grundig small black: 92.6%, see 5.16) with already very high values. Most of the issues when performing a task deal with problems to identify the "volume" or "channel up" button that were implemented on the remote controls with different icons. For instance the "increase volume" button on the Grundig large black remote control is realised as a button labelled "+". Similar as the result of the mobile phone user trial, this leads to the suggestion to use universal labelling on buttons if possible.

## Washing Machines

This section is structured into five parts: General comments from expert evaluation of both washing machine panels, recommendation checklist by expert, results of the user study with beneficiaries, panel comparison by beneficiaries and panel comparison by expert. The Arçelik Washing Machine Panels were not available on time, so an expert accessibility evaluation was conducted on them.

| Positive | Negative |
|---|---|
| • Clear typeface.<br>• Good colour contrast between buttons and their surrounding.<br>• Matt finish on buttons.<br>• Visual appearance of program selection knob is good.<br>• Visually clear and tactile marking on program selection knob.<br>• Audible and tactile "click" from all major and minor controls on activation, except the temperature button (although this may be the result of damage to the display).<br>• Good large size to the detergent drawer with enough space for any sized hand to fit in. | • It is difficult to know what to do first. Do you press "On"? Or do you select a program? Why is an "On" button necessary at all? What is the difference between Start/Pause/Cancel and On/Off?<br>• Avoid bold and italics in labels.<br>• It is not clear why some program labels are in bold, italics and purple text, while others are in regular grey text.<br>• Glossy finish on button surround.<br>• No obvious audible or tactile "click" from the temperature button on activation.<br>• Parallax issues: the user has to kneel in front of the display in order to read the full program guide (the program selection knob blocks the view of the bottom programs).<br>• For a quick wash, does the user select "Express 39" from the program guide or "Quick Wash" from the minor controls? What is the difference?<br>• There is no "home" setting for the program selection knob. This means that the starting point for the knob might be different every time the user puts on a wash. For users who count the turns, in order to find the desired program this is a particular issue. |

Table 5.17: General Comments - Arçelik Washing Machine Panel 1 - Part A

| Positive | Negative |
|---|---|
| | • The program selection knob is too difficult to turn. |
| | • The program selection knob does not give any tactile feedback when turned. |
| | • The start button is hard to press. |
| | • The on/off button is hard to press. |
| | • The start button is a critical button which the user will use every single time the washing machine is in use, but it is hidden amongst the other controls. |
| | • The location of the buttons relative to the order in which you use them is not intuitive. The user presses "On" (on the right), then selects a program (to the left), then selects one or more of the minor controls (to the left), then presses "Start" (to the right). The layout should more closely mirror the user journey. |
| | • Difficult to press and hold the Start/Pause/Cancel button for three seconds. |
| | • The "Cancel" label is mid-way between two different controls. Spacing should be used so that there is no confusion between buttons and their corresponding labels. |
| | • The "+" button must be pressed repeatedly to increase the time delay in increments of 5 minutes. |

Table 5.18: General Comments - Arçelik Washing Machine Panel 1 - Part B

| Positive | Negative |
|---|---|
| • Clear typeface. <br><br> • Visually clear and tactile marking on program selection knob. <br><br> • Large buttons. <br><br> • Good sized detergent drawer with enough space for any sized hand to fit in. | • It is difficult to know what to do first. Do you press "On"? Or do you select a program? Why is an "On" button necessary at all? <br><br> • What is the difference between Start/Pause/Cancel and On/Off? <br><br> • No colour contrast between buttons and their surround. <br><br> • High gloss finish on buttons and their surround. <br><br> • Avoid bold and italics in labels. <br><br> • It is not clear why some program labels are in bold and italics, while others are in regular grey text. <br><br> • No audible and tactile "click" from any of the major or minor controls on activation. <br><br> • Parallax issues: the user has to kneel in front of the display in order to read the full program guide (the program selection knob blocks the view of the bottom programs). <br><br> • For a quick wash, does the user select "Express 39" from the program guide or "Quick Wash" from the minor controls? What is the difference? <br><br> • The names of some of the programs are not intuitive - "Rinse" on the program selection knob versus "Rinse Plus" on the minor controls? <br><br> • There is no "home" setting for the program selection knob. This means that the starting point for the knob might be different every time the user puts on a wash. For users who count the turns, in order to find the desired program this is a particular issue. |

Table 5.19: General Comments - Arçelik Washing Machine Panel 2 - Part A

| Positive | Negative |
|---|---|
| | • The Start/Pause/Cancel label is too close to the program labels. |
| | • The program selection knob is too difficult to turn. |
| | • The program selection knob does not give any tactile feedback when turned. |
| | • The program selection knob can sit between two programs. |
| | • The on/off button is difficult to press. |
| | • The start button is a critical button which the user will use every single time the washing machine is in use, but it is hidden amongst the other controls. |
| | • The location of the buttons relative to the order in which you use them is not intuitive. The user presses "On" (on the right), then selects a program (to the left), then selects one or more of the minor controls (to the left), then presses "Start" (to the right). The layout should more closely mirror the user journey. |
| | • Difficult to press and hold the Start/Pause/Cancel button for three seconds. |
| | • The "Cancel" label is mid-way between two different controls. Spacing should be used so that there is no confusion between buttons and their corresponding labels. |
| | • The "+" button must be pressed repeatedly to increase the time delay in increments of 5 minutes. |
| | • The labels are already wearing off. |
| | • Inconsistent font size on the program selection knob labels. |
| | • The program selection knob is very cluttered with 16 program options. |

Table 5.20: General Comments - Arçelik Washing Machine Panel 2 - Part B

The side-by-side comparison regarding washing machines was conducted by a user study but also by an accessibility expert of NCBI[1]. In the first comparison (see table 5.27) no accessibility issues were solved from existing to emerged user interface but one new issue appeared with respect to a smaller selection knob. The second comparison by the expert figured out, that one accessibility issue regarding the distance between the + and - button was solved, but with the modification 10 new issues appeared (see tables 5.28 and 5.29).

On the contrary, in the user trials the washing machine panel 2 performance (73.43%) was slightly better than panel 1 (68.75%, see table 5.26). The reason of this lies in the amount of problems with labelling. While issues regarding the labelling only count as one single accessibility issue, they do have a much higher impact in practical use.
With respect to the software, this recommends a high importance for accessibility to have good and easy readable labels. In the recommendation list provided, label accessibility issues can be found in several recommendations (R-02, R-04, R-14 etc.).

This part of the evaluation also covers a comparison of output of the framework with the real prototype design. Recommendation lists provided by the framework were compared with the Doro Mock-Up phone (see table 5.13), if the recommendations were applied correctly or not. One issue not included in the Mock-Up relates to holding issue of beneficiaries with a weak grip. Since the material of the Doro Mock-Up phone and so weight and surface material of the functioning phone was not available, results (10 of 12 issues for Doro Mock-Up) show that recommendations were almost properly applied.

## 5.3.5 Discussion

This part of the evaluation also covered a comparison of output of the framework with the real prototype design. Recommendation lists were compared to the Doro Mock-Up phone, Arçelik washing machine panel 1 and 2 by an expert (see tables 5.13, 5.21, 5.22, 5.23, 5.24 and 5.25), if the recommendations were applied correctly or not. The results (10/12 for Doro Mock-Up, 20/25 Arçelik washing machine panel 1 and 14/25 Arçelik washing machine panel 2) show that some recommendations were not properly applied. This issue can also be identified in the side-by-side comparison results as seen in table 5.27. As already mentioned, the Arçelik washing machine panel 2 is a prototype in which one single recommendation of the framework

---

[1]See focus group report of the VICON project Vicon Consortium [2013b])

| Recommendation | Result |
|---|---|
| **Controls** | |
| Good visual contrast between the keys and the appliance - Major controls | Pass |
| Good visual contrast between the keys and the appliance - Minor controls | Pass / Room for improvement |
| Key tops should be convex or flat with a raised edge. | Pass |
| Keys should be as large as possible without reducing the distance between the keys to less than half the key width. | Pass |
| Ideally the keys should be internally illuminated, but the internal illumination should not reduce the legibility. | Fail |
| The visual markings on the keys should be high contrast, clear, and as large as is possible on the key top. | Pass / Room for improvement |
| The pressure to activate a key should be between 0.5 and 1 Newton. | N/A |
| There should be auditory and tactual feedback of control activation. | Pass |
| For controls that do not have any physical travel, audio or tactile feedback should be provided so the user knows when the control has been activated (e.g. a toggle switch or a push-in/pop-out switch). | Pass |
| There is a clearly labelled reset control. | N/A |
| Buttons, or keys have tactile markings. | Pass / Room for improvement |
| Buttons, or keys (including touch screen buttons) are large and easily identifiable from each other. | Pass |
| Buttons or keys are operable with one hand. | Pass |
| Glare is minimised on the surface of the product | Fail |
| **Instructions (Program Guide)** | |
| Use simple clear concise language. | Fail |
| Be task orientated. | Pass |
| Use a typeface with good legibility. | Pass, but bold and italics should not be used |
| **Labelling** | |
| Symbols should be accompanied by text. | Pass / Room for improvement |
| Symbols should be easily recognisable. | Pass / Room for improvement |
| The text and background colour combination should have high contrast. | Pass |
| A clear open typeface (font) should be used for text. | Pass |

Table 5.21: Recommendation Checklist of Arçelik Washing Machine Panel 1 - Part A

| Recommendation | Result |
|---|---|
| **Labelling** (continued from Part A) | |
| Text should not be placed over a background image or over a patterned background. | Pass |
| White or yellow type on black or a dark colour is more legible. | Fail |
| The typeface weight and size are suitable. | Pass / Room for improvement |
| Upper and lower case is used. | Pass |
| **Washing Machines** | |
| Minimum strength is needed to open and close the door. | N/A |
| Controls are easy to grip and turn. | Fail, easy to grip but stiff to turn |
| The door opens flat or as wide as possible for maximum access. | N/A |
| The dome in the door does not provide an obstruction to access. | N/A |
| Wheels are added for ease of moving top loading machines. | N/A |
| The door handle or button is easily activated. | N/A |
| The drawer for the soap powder is fairly large. | Pass |
| Noise emission is at a minimum level. | N/A |
| **Result** | **20/25** |

Table 5.22: Recommendation Checklist of Arçelik Washing Machine Panel 1 - Part B

| Recommendation | Result |
|---|---|
| **Controls** | |
| Good visual contrast between the keys and the appliance - Major controls | Fail |
| Good visual contrast between the keys and the appliance - Minor controls | Fail |
| Key tops should be convex or flat with a raised edge. | Pass |
| Keys should be as large as possible without reducing the distance between the keys to less than half the key width. | Pass |
| Ideally the keys should be internally illuminated, but the internal illumination should not reduce the legibility. | Fail |
| The visual markings on the keys should be high contrast, clear, and as large as is possible on the key top. | Fail |
| The pressure to activate a key should be between 0.5 and 1 Newton. | N/A |

Table 5.23: Recommendation Checklist of Arçelik Washing Machine Panel 2 - Part A

| Recommendation | Result |
|---|---|
| **Controls** (continued from Part A) | |
| There should be auditory and tactual feedback of control activation. | Fail |
| For controls that do not have any physical travel, audio or tactile feedback should be provided so the user knows when the control has been activated (e.g. a toggle switch or a push-in/pop-out switch). | Fail |
| There is a clearly labelled reset control. | N/A |
| Buttons, or keys have tactile markings. | Fail |
| Buttons, or keys (including touch screen buttons) are large and easily identifiable from each other. | Pass |
| Buttons or keys are operable with one hand. | Pass |
| Glare is minimised on the surface of the product | Fail |
| **Instructions (Program Guide)** | |
| Use simple clear concise language. | Fail |
| Be task orientated. | Pass |
| Use a typeface with good legibility. | Pass, but bold and italics should not be used |
| **Labelling** | |
| Symbols should be accompanied by text. | Pass / Room for improvement |
| Symbols should be easily recognisable. | Pass / Room for improvement |
| The text and background colour combination should have high contrast. | Pass |
| A clear open typeface (font) should be used for text. | Pass |
| Text should not be placed over a background image or over a patterned background. | Pass |
| White or yellow type on black or a dark colour is more legible. | Fail |
| The typeface weight and size are suitable. | Pass / Room for improvement |
| Upper and lower case is used. | Pass |
| **Washing Machines** | |
| Minimum strength is needed to open and close the door. | N/A |
| Controls are easy to grip and turn. | Fail, easy to grip but stiff to turn |
| The door opens flat or as wide as possible for maximum access. | N/A |
| The dome in the door does not provide an obstruction to access. | N/A |
| Wheels are added for ease of moving top loading machines. | N/A |

Table 5.24: Recommendation Checklist of Arçelik Washing Machine Panel 2 - Part B

| Recommendation | Result |
|---|---|
| **Washing Machines** (continued from Part B) | |
| The door handle or button is easily activated. | N/A |
| The drawer for the soap powder is fairly large. | Pass |
| Noise emission is at a minimum level. | N/A |
| **Result** | **14/25** |

Table 5.25: Recommendation Checklist of Arçelik Washing Machine Panel 2 - Part C

| Task | Arçelik Washing Machine Panel 1 | Arçelik Washing Machine Panel 2 |
|---|---|---|
| Identify the "on/off" button | 8/8 | 8/8 |
| Push "on/off" button | 6/8 | 6/8 |
| Identify the set Program | 8/8 | 8/8 |
| Turn knob to set Program | 2/8 | 2/8 |
| Identify main control panel | 8/8 | 8/8 |
| Read and understand texts of main panel | 2/8 | 3/8 |
| Identify minor control panel | 8/8 | 8/8 |
| Read and understand texts of minor panel | 2/8 | 4/8 |
| **Total** | 68.75% | 73.43% |

Table 5.26: Results of user study regarding washing machines

| Difficulty encountered | Arçelik Existing Panel 1 | Arçelik Mock-up Panel 2 |
|---|---|---|
| **Cognitive features** | | |
| Meaning of labels is not intuitive | Yes | Yes |
| Technical terminology used | Yes | Yes |
| **Sensory features** | | |
| Difficulty reading the labels | Yes | Yes |
| Difficult to find programs | Yes | Yes |
| **Physical features** | | |
| "On/off" button is hard to press | Yes | Yes |
| Program selection knob difficult to turn | Yes | Yes |
| Program selection knob is too small to hold and control | No | Yes |
| **Total number of issues** | **6** | **7** |

Table 5.27: Result comparison regarding washing machines by user study

| Difficulty encountered | Arçelik Existing Panel 1 | Arçelik Mock-up Panel 2 |
|---|---|---|
| **Cognitive features** | | |
| Order of use not intuitive | Yes | Yes |
| Meaning of labels not intuitive | Yes | Yes |
| Technical terminology used | Yes | Yes |
| Meaning of formatting is unclear (why some labels are in bold and italics, others are not) | Yes | Yes |
| **Sensory features** | | |
| Bold and italics used in labels | Yes | Yes |
| Glossy finish on button surround | Yes | Yes |
| Glossy finish on button | No | Yes |
| No obvious audible click from buttons | No | Yes |
| No obvious tactile click from buttons | No | Yes |
| Parallax issues (user needs to bend down to read lower control labels, as the knob blocks view) | Yes | Yes |
| Start button is "hidden" among the other controls | Yes | Yes |
| Start label is too close to program guide labels | No | Yes |
| Cancel label is midway between two buttons | Yes | Yes |
| Poor visual contrast between label and surround | Yes | Yes |
| No colour contrast between buttons and surround | No | Yes |
| Program selection knob cluttered | No | Yes (16 programs, versus 12 on Panel 1) |
| Labels wearing off (Note: this may be due to the fact that it is a prototype) | No | Yes |
| **Physical features** | | |
| "On/off" button is hard to press | Yes | Yes |
| Start button is hard to press | Yes | Yes |
| Difficult to hold and press "Start" button for three seconds | Yes | Yes |
| Program selection knob difficult to turn | Yes | Yes |

Table 5.28: Result comparison regarding washing machines by expert - Part A

| Difficulty encountered | Arçelik Existing Panel 1 | Arçelik Mock-up Panel 2 |
|---|---|---|
| **Physical features** (continued from Part A) | | |
| No "home" setting for the program selection knob, so the starting point will change. | Yes | Yes |
| Program selection knob does not give any tactile feedback on turning | No | Yes |
| Program selection knob can sit between two settings (i.e. does not click into place) | No | Yes |
| Difficult to press "+" button repeatedly | Yes | Yes |
| "+" and "-" buttons too close together | Yes | No |
| Inconsistent font size on program selection knob | No | Yes |
| **Total number of issues** | **17** | **26** |

Table 5.29: Result comparison regarding washing machines by expert - Part B

was solved, resulting in new accessibility issues.

As a result with respect to the hypothesis 3.3 the following issues were resolved:

- The use of product interfaces relies on readable and understandable labelling information, so recommendations regarding labels and text information are very important.

  Results of the study show a product can only be as much accessible as the user understands the features. Country-specific terminology or pictograms must be evaluated and applied to product interfaces for accessibility and a better comprehension by customers.

- It is not advantageous to concern only one single recommendation, all issues must be solved for a product to be more inclusive, otherwise the modification can also imply new accessibility issues.

  The coverage of each different recommendation is important. If only one single recommendation is covered, even new accessibility issues can appear as seen regarding washing machine panels. Therefore recommendations can be functions of each other.

- If all recommendations are included, product interfaces can be used by a wider group of people.

This issue was one main result of this part of the evaluation, as recommendations were in line with recommendations given by the expert but also recommendations stated by customers.

## 5.4 Conclusion

The aim of this thesis is to contribute in research by creating a solution for supporting product designers during the product development process. The solution was implemented as a supportive framework including different tools for designers (as seen in chapter 4). To evaluate the complete framework and especially the benefit of the framework, hypothesis 3 was separated into three sub-hypotheses. Due to the impact of the framework on the product development process the first sub-hypothesis 3.1 stated to support designers to create more inclusive designed products. The evaluation was conducted as interviews about opinions and knowledge of designers if the concept was suitable for adaptation.

**Hypothesis 3 (*Designer acceptance*)**

*The involvement of context awareness for designers about impairments of product beneficiaries into different phases of product development provides adequate flexibility and designer acceptance by requirement traceability due to the focus of each phase upon different scenario issues.*

Three main issues were identified from this study:

- The system is as useful as data and recommendations provided. This issue resolves the fact that there is a strong connection between output data and usability in existing product development processes. It is very important to have an as brought expanse of recommendations as possible to cover all relevant aspects of inclusive design.

- With the system it is possible to prevent conceptional and usability faults before prototyping. Mostly in sketch design phase this issue infers additional information about end user requirements, which were or could not be covered in this early state. The benefit to have an impact already in the first design phase prevents design mistakes as early as possible before virtual or physical prototyping.

- It does not necessarily lead to an acceleration, but can also result in a deceleration of the design process due to product customization to user needs. Regarding modifications of the target product with respect to end user requirements, the fact to have customer information in an early stage must not necessarily result in a acceleration but can also result in a deceleration of the product development process. The creative process of design to cover issues regarding accessibility can decrease the speed of the design process but can also lead to more inclusive products. This issue is relevant especially when there are no suitable solutions to accessibility issues yet.

The second sub-hypothesis 3.2 expands the evaluation to the practical use of the framework in real product development processes and focuses on the suitability to support designers during product development without hindrance. Product designers were able to install and test the software framework in their typical environment to validate if the support is productive and can be included in existing processes without hindrance to typical design tasks. Results show a positive acceptance by designers even throughout different user involvement methods as presented in chapter 2.4.

In conclusion, two main issues were identified:

- The software is suitable to be included in existing product development processes independently of the user involvement method applied:
  All seven different customer involvement methods were covered by participants of the study as presented in section 5.2. Although the acceptance by designers depends on the output of recommendations, it is necessary for better acceptance to extend the amount of recommendations.

- An improvement regarding more comprehensive scenario information is advantageous:
  Regarding a more sophisticated scenario comprehension more background information is needed. This improvement can be made by an extended user manual including background information or a further presentation in the software framework.

The last sub-hypothesis adds the perspective of product customers by comparing emerged products created using the system with existing ones. In addition, an expert evaluation was conducted to rate the accessibility compared to recommendations given by the system. The comparison and the expert study identified the following issues:

- The use of product interfaces relies on readable and understandable labelling information, so recommendations regarding labels and text information are very important.
  Participants have had several problems regarding the identification of single

functions with respect to their icons or characteristics. For instance the "SMS" button on mobile phones could not be identified correctly in Ireland as it is not commonly used for messages as e.g. in Germany. Icons instead lead to overcome barriers related to language or literacy but the functional meaning of logos can also be ambiguous.

- It is not advantageous to concern only one single recommendation, all issues must be solved for a product to be more inclusive, otherwise the modification can also imply new accessibility issues.

  This issue was raised regarding the washing machine panels, in which one single recommendation was solved, but 10 new accessibility issues appeared.

- If all recommendations are included, product interfaces can be used by a wider group of people.

  Most participants were satisfied with the new accessibility and stated the same recommendations as the system.

The evaluation concludes a positive feedback from both perspectives designers and end customers, but with additional comments. The system is capable to be included into real product development processes and does not affect existing product development processes as an obstacle in typical product design. Also a strong learning curve was observed, raising context awareness of end customers on designer side. However a broad expanse of recommendations regarding product interaction is required helping designer in the creation of suitable inclusive design for an as wide group of end customers as possible.

# Chapter 6

# Discussion and Future Work

## 6.1 Discussion

The aim of this thesis was a contribution to support product designers during the product development process solving the problem of inclusion of beneficiary needs. More precisely designers should be able to access contextual information about customers of their product to include related issues as early as possible. A framework was implemented and applied in industrial field.

The data used in the system has to be widely extended, so also cognitive impairments can be included by the addition of new classes and rules analogously as existing impairment profiles described in section 3.2.1 and 3.4.4. Regarding the definition of cognitive parameters and the classification of User Models into no, mild and moderate cognitive impairment groups, user trials are necessary. Also different new target products can be implemented.

One main factor during this thesis was the software not restraining the designer. A possible software framework would add the possibility for designers to create a virtual model of their product, press one big "Start" button and afterwards the product is inclusive. The software would change the complete design to end user needs itself. On the one side, it would be great to have such a solution, but this would also result in a smaller variety of product designs. Each product would only focus on the connection of technological and human factors by guidelines and conditions. This extreme scenario results in inclusive design, but would also destroy creativity during product development process. The amount of different designs would be narrowed by the target device, resulting in very similar end results.

The presented framework can be seen as a first supportive concept regarding inclusive design and was proven that it already can help during product development processes. But for a seamless integration without restrictions even to devices, a hierarchical superstructure about various kinds of interactions is necessary. As seen in section 1.1, during the last years technology evolved due to new functional possibilities but also new kinds of interaction (speech, gesture etc.). For instance buttons are increasingly replaced by touchscreens both reflecting the same functionality. Different devices can provide the same functionality.

It is possible to include a higher stage of hierarchy into the framework presented in this thesis, as different user tests would be necessary to obtain the information, which devices are suitable for which functionality.

When restricted to single devices, results using the presented framework can be optimal. Regarding a more idealistic view, an optimal scenario would be to get recommendations by target functionality (or functionalities).

The target functionality would be the main hierarchical root defining suitable devices. The current evolutions such as smart phones are in line with this theory. Existing devices could be selected by their suitability based on a set of target functionalities. Even new devices could be generated by need if a set of functionalities can not be provided by existing ones.

## 6.2 Future Work

As mentioned in chapter 3, the data used in the presented framework can be widely extended. The software is already used in industry and is available as open source[1]. A further development is advantageous especially due to the connection of functionality and device.

With respect to the software framework but also inclusive design, the following areas would be interesting:

- Standardisation of User Model

  The VUMS cluster prepared a position paper providing input to the standardisation of User Models. Based on User Models of the projects VERITAS, VICON, MyUI and GUIDE a standard definition of a representative virtual user including parameters for hearing, visual, manual dexterity and cognitive impairments was created (see VUMS White Paper[2]).

  Finally it targets at helping designers and developers to maximize the level of usability and accessibility of products and services by providing appropriate user models. Moreover they are intended to be used for the generation and adaptation of user interfaces during runtime. It presents general definitions and a

---

[1]SourceForge website: http://sourceforge.net/projects/convic/
[2]VUMS White Paper can be found at: http://veritas-project.eu/2012/02/vums-white-paper/

concept of generic interoperable user models that describe the relevant characteristics of users interacting with products and user interfaces. These include physical, cognitive, and sensory attributes, habits, preferences and accessibility capabilities.

- Extending to functionality as top hierarchy
A hierarchical superstructure of target functionalities as $n - m$ relations would be preferable especially if the design is not restricted to a device. If design is not restricted, interaction recommendations between human and computer would be possible. For instance the simple interaction of "reading and writing emails" would infer a display/keypad and a touch display for the same purpose. Both solutions could handle the task. Designers could select human-computer interactions and choose from a set of solutions. In addition, if there are new technological advancements, new devices could be included by provided functionality.

- Extension of recommendations
An extension of recommendations would always be preferable especially regarding new devices. In the current version recommendations focus on the interaction used by mobile phones, tv remotes and washing machine panels. There is a need to include new instances in the task model when extending the knowledge base to new devices.

- Inclusion of structured and annotated CAD objects
Regarding the CAD environment, the aim would be to describe "exemplary" CAD objects which could appear in the integrated module. Designers would be able to select single objects from a predefined and already inclusively created set of objects for new products. The reasoning would be able to present a subset of possible objects based on different conditions of the target product.

# References

C. Abbott. tiresias. org information resource for people working in the field of visual disabilities. *Journal of Assistive Technologies*, 1(1):58–59, 2007.

Y. Akao. *Quality function deployment: integrating customer requirements into product design*. Productivity Press, 2004.

Franz Baader. *The description logic handbook: theory, implementation, and applications*. Cambridge university press, 2003.

M. Baldauf, S. Dustdar, and F. Rosenberg. A survey on context-aware systems. *International Journal of Ad Hoc and Ubiquitous Computing*, 2(4):263–277, 2007.

A. Berthold. *Der fertigungsorientierte Modellierer FERMOD als Erweiterung des Konstruktionssystems WISKON*. PhD thesis, Kassel University, 2002.

Pradipta Biswas, Pat Langdon, Christoph Jung, Pascal Hamisu, Carlos Duarte, and Luis Almeida. Developing intelligent user interfaces for e-accessibility and e-inclusion. In *Proceedings of the 2012 ACM international conference on Intelligent User Interfaces*, IUI '12, pages 405–408, New York, NY, USA, 2012. ACM. ISBN 978-1-4503-1048-2. doi: 10.1145/2166966.2167060. URL http://doi.acm.org/10.1145/2166966.2167060.

BMW AG. BMW Website - BMW Techniklexikon : Controller. http://www.bmw.com/com/de/insights/technology/technology_guide/articles/controller.html?content_type=/com/de/insights/technology/technology_guide/articles/control_display.html&source=/com/de/insights/technology/technology_guide/articles/idrive.html&article=controller. Accessed: 2013-03-04.

Cardiac Consortium. Advancing research & development in the area of accessible and assistive ict. http://www.cardiac-eu.org/, 2012.

J. Cassim and H. Dong. Empowering designers and users: Case studies from the dba inclusive design challenge. *Design for inclusivity: a practical guide to accessible, innovative and user-centred design*, page 89, 2007.

E. Castillo and E. Alvarez. *Expert systems: uncertainty and learning.* WIT Press, 1991.

E. Castillo, J.M. Gutiérrez, and A.S. Hadi. *Expert systems and probabilistic network models.* Springer Verlag, 1997.

Eleni Chalkia, Evangelos Bekiaris, Karel Van Isacker, Serge Boverie, Onorino Di Tanna, Nikos Partarakis, Kostas Moustakas, Hans-Joachim Wirsching, Maria Fernanda Cabrera, Elena Tamburini, and Mytas Nicolas. Accessible and assistive ict - veritas deliverable 1.7.1 final - use cases and application scenarios, 2010.

S. Ciccantelli and J. Magidson. From experience: consumer idealized design: involving consumers in the product development process. *Journal of Product Innovation Management*, 10(4):341–347, 1993.

J. Clarkson. *Inclusive design: Design for the whole population.* Springer Verlag, 2003.

J. Clarkson, R. Coleman, S. Keates, and C. Lebbon. A designer-centred approach. *Inclusive design: Design for the whole population*, 2003.

R. Coleman and C. Lebbon. Inclusive design. *Helen Hamlyn Research Centre, Royal College of Art*, 2005.

R. Davis, B. Buchanan, and E. Shortliffe. Production rules as a representation for a knowledge-based consultation program. *Artificial intelligence*, 8(1):15–45, 1977.

H. Dong, S. Keates, and P. Clarkson. Inclusive design in industry: barriers, drivers and the business case. *User-Centered Interaction Paradigms for Universal Access in the Information Society*, pages 305–319, 2004.

H. Dong, P.J. Clarkson, J. Cassim, and S. Keates. Critical user forums-an effective user research method for inclusive design. *The Design Journal*, 8(2):49–59, 2005.

Vincent G. Duffy. *Handbook of Digital Human Modeling: Research for Applied Ergonomics and Human Factors Engineering.* CRC Press, Inc., Boca Raton, FL, USA, 1st edition, 2008. ISBN 0805856463, 9780805856460.

Inge E Eriks-Hoogland, Sonja de Groot, Marcel WM Post, and Lucas HV van der Woude. Passive shoulder range of motion impairment in spinal cord injury during and one year after rehabilitation. *Journal of Rehabilitation Medicine*, 41(6):438–444, 2009.

European Commission. Commission communication - the demographic future of europe - from challenge to opportunity. In *Europe in figures - Eurostat yearbook 2011*, 2011. URL http://eur-lex.europa.eu/LexUriServ/LexUriServ.do?uri=COM:2006:0571:FIN:EN:PDF.

M.R. Fine. *Beta testing for better software*. Wiley, 2002.

Charles L Forgy. Rete: A fast algorithm for the many pattern/many object pattern match problem. *Artificial intelligence*, 19(1):17–37, 1982.

Wireless Application Protocol Forum. Wag uaprof - version 20-oct-2001 - wireless application protocol wap-248-uaprof-20011020-a. In *WAP Forum, October*, volume 10, 2001.

B. Funke and H.J. Sebastian. *Knowledge-based model building with KONWERK*. Internat. Inst. for Applied Systems Analysis, 1996.

J.C. Giarratano and G. Riley. *Expert systems*. PWS Publishing Co., 1998.

John Gill. Access prohibited? *Information for Designers of Public Access Terminals, Royal National Institute for the Blind*, 224, 1997.

J. Goodman, H. Dong, P. Langdon, and P. Clarkson. Factors involved in industry's response to inclusive design. *Designing accessible technology*, pages 31–39, 2006a.

J. Goodman, PM Langdon, and PJ Clarkson. Providing strategic user information for designers: methods and initial findings. *Designing accessible technology*, pages 41–51, 2006b.

K. Goodwin. Getting from research to personas: Harnessing the power of data. *Cooper Newsletter*, 2002.

GUIDE Consortium. User Initialization application - Prototype. `http://www.guide-project.eu/index.php?mainItem=Publications&subItem=Project+Deliverables&pageNumber=1&item=38`, a. Accessed: 2013-08-21.

GUIDE Consortium. User Simulator Prototype. `http://www.guide-project.eu/index.php?mainItem=Publications&subItem=Project+Deliverables&pageNumber=1&item=22`, b. Accessed: 2013-08-21.

Guide Consortium. Project Deliverable 7.1: Initial User Tests and Model, 2011.

A. Günter and L. Hotz. Konwerk-a domain independent configuration tool. In *Configuration Papers from the AAAI Workshop*, pages 10–19, 1999.

HM Haines, JR Wilson, Health, and Nottingham (United Kingdom); Safety Executive, London (United Kingdom); Institute for Occupational Ergonomics. *Development of a framework for participatory ergonomics*. Sudbury: HSE Books, 1998.

T.A. Halpin, A.J. Morgan, and T. Morgan. *Information modeling and relational databases*. Morgan Kaufmann, 2008.

P. Hamisu, G. Heinrich, C. Jung, V. Hahn, C. Duarte, P. Langdon, and P. Biswas. Accessible ui design and multimodal interaction through hybrid tv platforms: towards a virtual-user centered design framework. *Universal Access in Human-Computer Interaction. Users Diversity*, pages 32–41, 2011.

F. Hayes-Roth, D. Waterman, and D. Lenat. *Building expert systems*. Addison-Wesley, Reading, MA, 1984.

A. Held, S. Buchholz, and A. Schill. Modeling of context information for pervasive computing applications. *Procceding of the World Multiconference on Systemics, Cybernetics and Informatics*, 2002.

K. Henricksen, J. Indulska, and T. McFadden. Modelling context information with orm. In *On the Move to Meaningful Internet Systems 2005: OTM 2005 Workshops*, pages 626–635. Springer, 2005.

C. Herstatt and E. Von Hippel. From experience: Developing new product concepts via the lead user method: A case study in a "low-tech" field. *Journal of product innovation management*, 9(3):213–221, 1992.

Human Solutions GmbH. Documentation of the RAMSIS Software. `http://www.appliedgroup.com/ramsis/`, 2012. Accessed: 2012-08-28.

Robert J Ivnik, James F Malec, Eric G Tangalos, Ronald C Petersen, Emre Kokmen, and Leonard T Kurland. The auditory-verbal learning test (avlt): norms for ages 55 years and older. *Psychological Assessment: A Journal of Consulting and Clinical Psychology*, 2(3):304, 1990.

C. Jung and V. Hahn. Guide-adaptive user interfaces for accessible hybrid tv applications. In *Second W3C Workshop Web & TV*, 2011.

Nikolaos Kaklanis, Panagiotis Moschonas, Konstantinos Moustakas, and Dimitrios Tzovaras. Enforcing accessible design of products and services through simulated accessibility evaluation. *Tangible Information Technology for a Better Ageing Society*, page 59, 2010.

Nikolaos Kaklanis, Yehya Mohamad, Matthias Peissner, Pradipta Biswas, Patrick Langdon, and Dimitrios Tzovaras. An interoperable and inclusive user modelling concept for simulation and adaptation. In *UMAP Workshops*, 2012a.

Nikolaos Kaklanis, Panagiotis Moschonas, Konstantinos Moustakas, and Dimitrios Tzovaras. Virtual user models for the elderly and disabled for automatic simulated accessibility and ergonomy evaluation of designs. *Universal Access in the Information Society*, pages 1–23, 2012b. ISSN 1615-5289. doi: 10.1007/s10209-012-0281-0. URL `http://dx.doi.org/10.1007/s10209-012-0281-0`.

Tapas Kanungo, David M Mount, Nathan S Netanyahu, Christine D Piatko, Ruth Silverman, and Angela Y Wu. An efficient k-means clustering algorithm: Analysis and implementation. *Pattern Analysis and Machine Intelligence, IEEE Transactions on*, 24(7):881–892, 2002.

M.A. Kaulio. Customer, consumer and user involvement in product development: A framework and a review of selected methods. *Total Quality Management*, 9(1): 141–149, 1998.

Mohsen Kazemi. Adhesive capsulitis: a case report. *The Journal of the Canadian Chiropractic Association*, 44(3):169, 2000.

S. Keates, P.J. Clarkson, L.A. Harrison, and P. Robinson. Towards a practical inclusive design approach. In *Proceedings on the 2000 conference on Universal Usability*, pages 45–52. ACM, 2000.

M. Kifer. Rule interchange format: The framework. *Web reasoning and rule systems*, pages 1–11, 2008.

Michael Kifer. rule interchange format: logic programming's second wind? In *Proceedings of the 20th international conference on Inductive logic programming*, ILP'10, pages 1–1, Berlin, Heidelberg, 2011. Springer-Verlag. ISBN 978-3-642-21294-9. URL http://dl.acm.org/citation.cfm?id=2022735.2022737.

P. Kirisci, P. Klein, M. Modzelewski, M. Lawo, Y. Mohamad, T. Fiddian, C. Bowden, A. Fennell, and J. Connor. Supporting inclusive design of user interfaces with a virtual user model. *Universal Access in Human-Computer Interaction. Users Diversity*, pages 69–78, 2011a.

P.T. Kirisci, K.D. Thoben, P. Klein, and M. Modzelewski. Supporting inclusive product design with virtual user models at the early stages of product development. In *Proceedings of the 18th International Conference on Engineering Design (ICED11)*, *Vol. 9*, pages 80–90, 2011b.

C. Kiss. Composite capability/preference profiles (cc/pp): Structure and vocabularies 2.0. *W3C Working Draft*, 8, 2006.

Pat Langdon. Developing an interactive tv for the elderly and impaired: An inclusive design strategy. In Pradipta Biswas, Carlos Duarte, Patrick Langdon, Luis Almeida, and Christoph Jung, editors, *A Multimodal End-2-End Approach to Accessible Computing*, Human–Computer Interaction Series, pages 23–48. Springer London, 2013. ISBN 978-1-4471-5081-7. doi: 10.1007/978-1-4471-5082-4_2. URL http://dx.doi.org/10.1007/978-1-4471-5082-4_2.

Patrick Langdon and Harold Thimbleby. Inclusion and interaction: Designing inter-action for inclusive populations. *Interacting with Computers*, 22(6):439–448, 2010.

P.M. Langdon and P. Biswas. Clustering user data for user modelling in the guide multi-modal set-top box. In Patrick Langdon, John Clarkson, Peter Robinson, Jonathan Lazar, and Ann Heylighen, editors, *Designing Inclusive Systems*, pages 195–204. Springer London, 2012. ISBN 978-1-4471-2866-3. doi: 10.1007/978-1-4471-2867-0_20. URL http://dx.doi.org/10.1007/978-1-4471-2867-0_20.

Ora Lassila, Ralph R. Swick, World Wide, and Web Consortium. Resource description framework (rdf) model and syntax specification, 1998.

M. Lawo, P. Kirisci, M. Modzelewski, J. O'Connor, A. Fennell, T. Fiddian, H. Gökmen, M. Klann, M. Geissler, S. Matiouk, and Y. Mohamad. Virtual user models – ap-proach and first results of the vicon project. *eChallenges e-2011 Conference Pro-ceedings*, 2011.

Rensis Likert. A technique for the measurement of attitudes. *Archives of psychology*, 1932.

Quentin Limbourg, Jean Vanderdonckt, Benjamin Michotte, Laurent Bouillon, and Víctor López-Jaquero. Usixml: A language supporting multi-path development of user interfaces. In *Engineering human computer interaction and interactive systems*, pages 200–220. Springer, 2005.

Robert K. Lindsay, Bruce G. Buchanan, Edward A. Feigenbaum, and Joshua Lederberg. Dendral: A case study of the first expert system for scientific hy-pothesis formation. *Artificial Intelligence*, 61(2):209 – 261, 1993. ISSN 0004-3702. doi: http://dx.doi.org/10.1016/0004-3702(93)90068-M. URL http://www.sciencedirect.com/science/article/pii/000437029390068M.

A. Martini. European working group on genetics of hearing impairment infoletter 2, european commission directorate. *Biomedical and Health Research Programme (HEAR)*, 1996.

Larry Masinter, Tim Berners-Lee, and Roy T Fielding. Uniform resource identifier (uri): Generic syntax. 2005.

Svetlana Matiouk, Markus Modzelewski, Yehya Mohamad, Michael Lawo, Pierre Kirisci, Patrick Klein, and Antoinette Fennell. Prototype of a virtual user model-ing software framework for inclusive design of consumer products and user inter-faces. In *Universal Access in Human-Computer Interaction. Design Methods, Tools, and Interaction Techniques for eInclusion*, pages 59–66. Springer, 2013.

B. McBride. Jena: A semantic web toolkit. *Internet Computing, IEEE*, 6(6):55–59, 2002.

Brian McBride. Jena: Implementing the rdf model and syntax specification. In *SemWeb*, 2001.

William L. Moore. Concept testing. *Journal of Business Research*, 10(3):279 – 294, 1982. ISSN 0148-2963. doi: 10.1016/0148-2963(82)90034-0. URL http://www.sciencedirect.com/science/article/pii/0148296382900340.

Panagiotis Moschonas, Athanasios Tsakiris, Nikolaos Kaklanis, Georgios Stavropoulos, and Dimitrios Tzovaras. Holistic accessibility evaluation using vr simulation of users with special needs. In *UMAP Workshops*, 2012.

A. Naumann and M. Roetting. Digital human modeling for design and evaluation of human-machine systems. *MMI-Interaktiv*, 12:27, 2007.

Alan F. Newell and Peter Gregor. User sensitive inclusive design - in search of a new paradigm. In *Proceedings on the 2000 conference on Universal Usability*, CUU '00, pages 39–44, New York, NY, USA, 2000. ACM. ISBN 1-58113-314-6. doi: 10.1145/355460.355470. URL http://doi.acm.org/10.1145/355460.355470.

World Health Organization et al. Deafness and hearing impairment. *See http://www.who.int/mediacentre/factsheets/fs300/en/index.html (last checked 12 Nov 2012)*, 2012a.

World Health Organization et al. Visual impairment and blindness. *See http://www.who.int/mediacentre/factsheets/fs282/en/index.html (last checked 12 Nov 2012)*, 2012b.

M. Peissner, A. Schuller, and D. Spath. A design patterns approach to adaptive user interfaces for users with special needs. *Human-Computer Interaction. Design and Development Approaches*, pages 268–277, 2011.

Matthias Peissner, Dagmar Häbe, Doris Janssen, and Thomas Sellner. Myui: generating accessible user interfaces from multimodal design patterns. In *Proceedings of the 4th ACM SIGCHI symposium on Engineering interactive computing systems*, EICS '12, pages 81–90, New York, NY, USA, 2012. ACM. ISBN 978-1-4503-1168-7. doi: 10.1145/2305484.2305500. URL http://doi.acm.org/10.1145/2305484.2305500.

Juan Carlos Peña-Guevara, Edmundo Berumen-Nafarrete, Arturo Aguirre-Madrid, Jorge Vallejo-Ponce, Ivanovish De la Riva-Muñoz, and Juan A Núñez-Valdez.

Anatomically-designed shoulder hemiarthroplasty made after 3-d models and implanted in a child with rheumatoid arthritis. a case report. *Acta Ortopédica Mexicana*, 19(1):S51–S55, 2005.

U. Persad, P. Langdon, and J. Clarkson. Characterising user capabilities to support inclusive design evaluation. *Universal Access in the Information Society*, 6(2):119–135, 2007.

B.J. Pine and S. Davis. *Mass customization: the new frontier in business competition.* Harvard Business School Pr, 1999.

Emilie Poirson and Matthieu Delangle. Comparative analysis of human modeling tools. 2013.

E. Prud'Hommeaux, A. Seaborne, et al. Sparql query language for rdf. *W3C recommendation*, 15, 2008.

Ralph M Reitan. *Trail Making Test: Manual for administration and scoring.* Reitan Neuropsychology Laboratory, 1986.

RNID. The Royal National Institute for Deaf People - VICON Task 2.1 - An overview, 2010. Presentation in Workshop Meeting, London, November 2010.

E. Rosenblad-Wallin. User-oriented product development applied to functional clothing design. *Applied Ergonomics*, 16(4):279–287, 1985.

James Rumbaugh, Ivar Jacobson, and Grady Booch. *Unified Modeling Language Reference Manual, The (2nd Edition).* Pearson Higher Education, 2004. ISBN 0321245628.

S.J. Russell and P. Norvig. *Artificial intelligence: a modern approach.* Prentice hall, 2010.

R.C. Schank and C.K. Riesbeck. *Inside computer understanding: Five programs plus miniatures.* Lawrence Erlbaum, 1981.

A. Schmidt and K. Van Laerhoven. How to build smart appliances? *Personal Communications, IEEE*, 8(4):66–71, 2001.

Wolfgang Schneider. *Ergonomische Gestaltung von Benutzungsschnittstellen: Kommentar zur Grundsatznorm DIN EN ISO 9241-110.* Beuth Verlag GmbH, 2008.

Sascha Segan. Enter the phablet: A history of phone-tablet hybrids. http://www.pcmag.com/slideshow/story/294004/enter-the-phablet-a-history-of-phone-tablet-hybrids, 2012.

E.H. Shortliffe. *Computer-based medical consultations: MYCIN*, volume 388. Elsevier New York, 1976.

Howard E Shrobe. Supporting and optimizing full unification in a forward chaining rule system. In *AAAI*, pages 710–715, 1993.

H. Snellen. *Dr. H. Snellen's Probebuchstaben zur Bestimmung der Sehschärfe*. H. Peters, 1863.

S. Staab and R. Studer. *Handbook on Ontologies*. Springer-Verlag Berlin Heidelberg, 2009.

T. Strang and C. Linnhoff-Popien. A context modeling survey. In *Workshop Proceedings*, 2004.

O. Strnad, A. Felic, and A. Schmidt. Context management für selbst-adaptive nutzer-schnittstellen am beispiel von myui. *Technik für ein selbstbestimmtes Leben*, 2012.

G. Stucki. International classification of functioning, disability, and health (icf): a promising framework and classification for rehabilitation medicine. *American journal of physical medicine & rehabilitation*, 84(10):733, 2005.

A. Sundin, M. Christmansson, and M. Larsson. A different perspective in participatory ergonomics in product development improves assembly work in the automotive industry. *International journal of industrial ergonomics*, 33(1):1–14, 2004.

The Apache Software Foundation. Reasoners and rule engines: Jena inference support. http://jena.apache.org/documentation/inference/, 2013.

VDI-Gesellschaft Entwicklung Konstruktion Vertrieb. VDI 2221, Methodik zum Entwickeln und Konstruieren Technischer Systeme und Produkte, 1993.

VDI-Gesellschaft Konstruktion und Entwicklung - Produktionstechnik (ADB) - Gemeinschaftsausschuß Produktplanung. VDI 2220, Produktplanung - Ablauf, Begriffe und Organisation, 1980.

VDI-Gesellschaft Konstruktion und Entwicklung - Produktionstechnik (ADB) - Gemeinschaftsausschuß Produktplanung. VDI 2223, Methodisches Entwerfen technischer Produkte. *Verein Deutscher Ingenieure: VDI-Handbuch Konstruktion, Berlin*, 2004.

Vicon Consortium. Project Deliverable 1.1: End user and environment field study, 2010.

Vicon Consortium. Project Deliverable 1.2 - Survey of Design Frameworks and Tools, 2010a.

Vicon Consortium. Project Deliverable 1.3 - Virtual Humans in a human-centred design process - a critical review, 2010b.

Vicon Consortium. Project Deliverable 1.4 - Functional and system requirements dossier, 2011a.

Vicon Consortium. Project Deliverable 3.1 - System Architecture and Interface Specification, 2011b.

Vicon Consortium. Project Deliverable 2.2 - Virtual User Model (Final release), 2012a.

Vicon Consortium. Project Deliverable 3.4 - Final prototype of the virtual user modelling software framework, 2012b.

Vicon Consortium. Project Deliverable 4.3 - Evaluation report on how convenient it is to use Virtual User Model and adapted prototype, 2013a.

Vicon Consortium. Project Deliverable 4.4 - Focus Group Report, 2013b.

H. Wache, T. Voegele, U. Visser, H. Stuckenschmidt, G. Schuster, H. Neumann, and S. Hübner. Ontology-based integration of information-a survey of existing approaches. In *IJCAI-01 workshop: ontologies and information sharing*, volume 2001, pages 108–117. Citeseer, 2001.

X.H. Wang, D.Q. Zhang, T. Gu, and H.K. Pung. Ontology based context modeling and reasoning using owl. In *Pervasive Computing and Communications Workshops, 2004. Proceedings of the Second IEEE Annual Conference on*, pages 18–22. IEEE, 2004.

D. Waterman. *A guide to expert systems*. Addison-Wesley Pub. Co., Reading, MA, 1986.

David Wechsler. Manual for the wechsler adult intelligence scale. 1955.

D.D. Woods. Decomposing automation: Apparent simplicity, real complexity. *Automation and human performance: Theory and applications*, pages 3–17, 1996.

KM Zackowski, AW Dromerick, SA Sahrmann, WT Thach, and AJ Bastian. How do strength, sensation, spasticity and joint individuation relate to the reaching deficits of people with chronic hemiparesis? *Brain*, 127(5):1035–1046, 2004.

W. Zhou, T. Armstrong, M. Reed, S. Hoffman, and D. Wegner. Simulating complex automotive assembly tasks using the humosim framework. *SAE Technical Paper*, pages 01–2279, 2009.

E. Zitkus, P. Langdon, and J. Clarkson. Accessibility evaluation: Assistive tools for design activity in product development. In *Proceedings on the 1st international conference on sustainable intelligent manufacturing*, pages 659–670, 2011.

# Appendix

## Graphs of Designer Tests

### General Questions

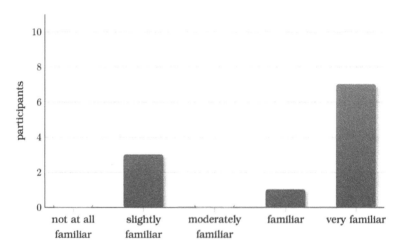

Figure 1: Personal knowledge of participants about design of physical products.

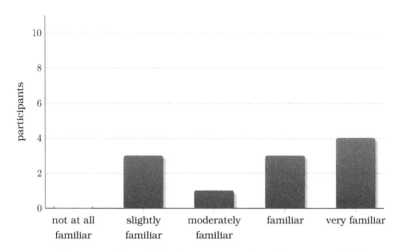

Figure 2: Personal knowledge of participants about Computer-aided Design.

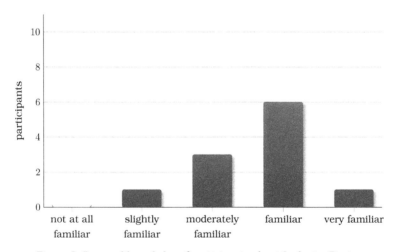

Figure 3: Personal knowledge of participants about Inclusive Design.

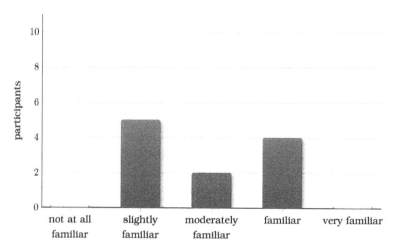

Figure 4: Personal knowledge of participants about Virtual User Modelling (VUM).

**Suitability for the task**

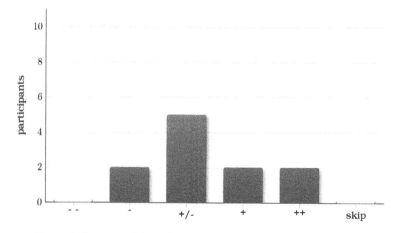

Figure 5: Question if the software provides a wide choice of scenarios.

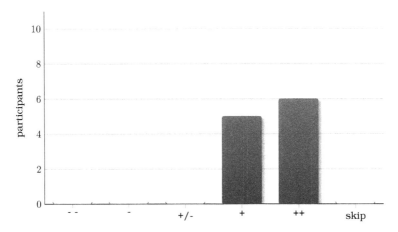

Figure 6: Question if the design recommendations of the toolset are necessary.

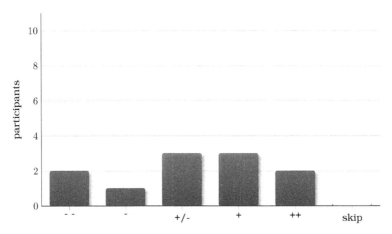

Figure 7: Question if it takes a short time to go through recommendation list.

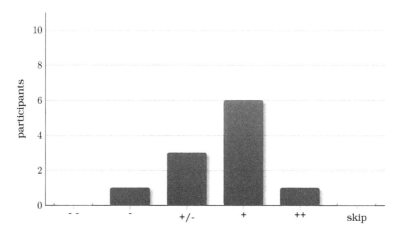

Figure 8: Question about the need of an user manual.

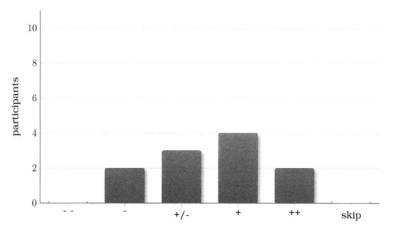

Figure 9: Question if the look and feel of the application is suitable and pleasant.

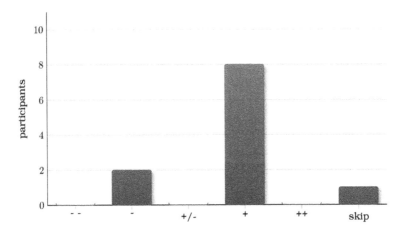

Figure 10: Question if the software is easy to use in general.

**Self-Descriptiveness**

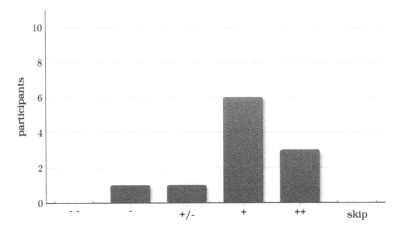

Figure 11: Question if the description of information in the sketch application for user profiles is comprehensible.

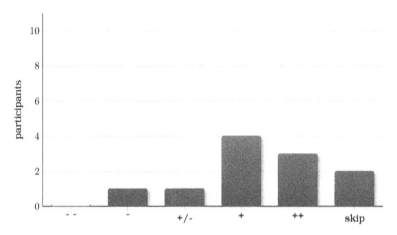

Figure 12: Question if the description of information in the sketch application for environments is comprehensible.

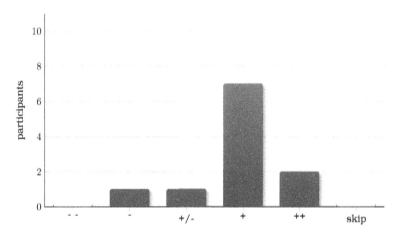

Figure 13: Question if the description of information in the sketch application for tasks is comprehensible.

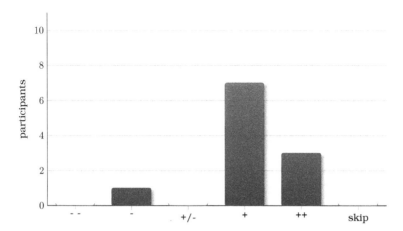

Figure 14: Question if the description about recommendations is comprehensible.

## Conformity with user expectations

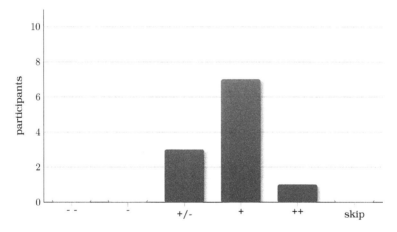

Figure 15: Question if from participant point of view the software has a consistent structure.

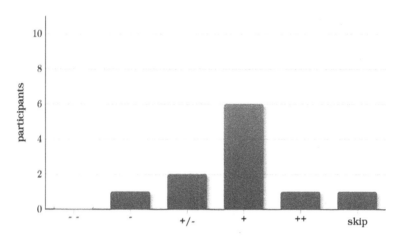

Figure 16: Question about layout expectations of the software.

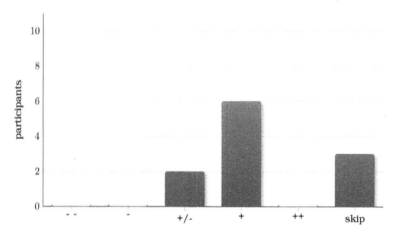

Figure 17: Question if some features of applications do not have an unpredictable processing time.

**Suitability for learning**

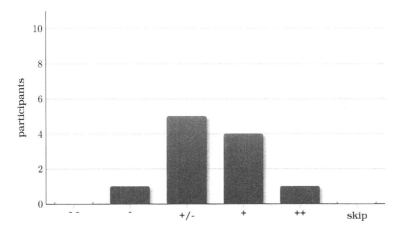

Figure 18: Question how much time is required for learning to use the software.

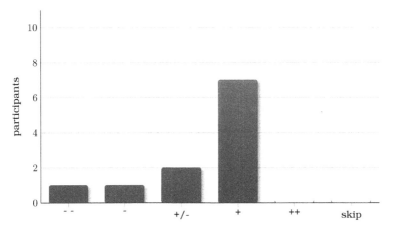

Figure 19: Question if the software is easy to learn without prior knowledge, help or manual.

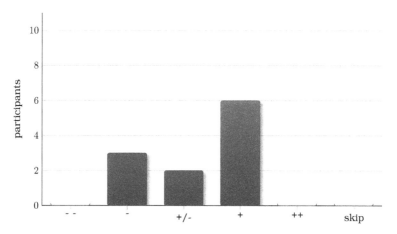

Figure 20: Question if the software is easy use to use, even without having prior knowledge.

## Complete Results of Beneficiary Tests

Source: Vicon Consortium [2013b]

### Profiles

| Age | Gender | Hearing | Vision | Manual Dexterity | Beneficiary Code (g=Germany, i=Ireland, t=Turkey |
|-----|--------|---------|--------|------------------|--------------------------------------------------|
| 65 | Female | Mild | Mild | No | g1 |
| 80 | Female | Mild | No | Moderate | g2 |
| 88 | Male | No | Severe[1] | Moderate | g3 |
| 73 | Female | No | No | Moderate | g4 |
| 88 | Female | Moderate | No | Mild | g5 |
| 94 | Female | Mild | No | No | g6 |
| 82 | Female | Moderate | No | Mild | g7 |
| 84 | Female | No | Moderate | Mild | g8 |
| 89 | Female | Mild | Moderate | Moderate | g9 |
| 70 | Female | Mild | Mild | No | g10 |

Continued on next page

---

[1]One beneficiary was deemed to have too severe a vision impairment to be included in the analysis, the total sample size therefore for the product analyses 47 instead of 48, see 5.3

| Age | Gender | Hearing | Vision | Manual Dexterity | Beneficiary Code (g=Germany, i=Ireland, t=Turkey |
|-----|--------|---------|--------|------------------|-----|
| 83 | Male | No | Mild | No | g11 |
| 80 | Female | No | Mild | No | g12 |
| 92 | Female | No | Mild | Moderate | g13 |
| 90 | Female | No | Moderate | Mild | g14 |
| 82 | Male | No | Moderate | No | g15 |
| 66 | Female | No | Moderate | No | g16 |
| 81 | Male | No | Moderate | Mild | g17 |
| 91 | Female | No | Mild | No | g18 |
| 76 | Female | No | Moderate | No | g19 |
| 87 | Female | No | Moderate | No | g20 |
| 74 | Female | Mild | Moderate | Mild | i1 |
| 88 | Male | Moderate | Mild | Mild | i2 |
| 90 | Female | Moderate | Moderate | Mild | i3 |
| 66 | Male | No | No | Mild | i4 |
| 84 | Female | Mild | Mild | No | i5 |
| 65 | Female | Moderate | Moderate | No | i6 |
| 65 | Male | Moderate | Moderate | No | i7 |
| 67 | Male | Mild | Mild | No | i8 |
| 65 | Female | No | Moderate | No | i9 |
| 68 | Male | Mild | Moderate | No | i10 |
| 75 | Female | No | Moderate | Mild | i11 |
| 78 | Male | Mild | Moderate | No | i12 |
| 70 | Female | No | Moderate | Mild | i13 |
| 81 | Female | Mild | Mild | No | i14 |
| 75 | Female | Moderate | Moderate | Moderate | i15 |
| 65 | Male | Mild | Mild | No | i16 |
| 65 | Female | No | Mild | Mild | i17 |
| 68 | Female | No | Mild | Mild | i18 |
| 79 | Female | Moderate | Moderate | No | i19 |
| 77 | Female | Mild | No | Moderate | i20 |
| 85 | Male | Mild | Mild | No | t1 |
| 73 | Female | No | Mild | No | t2 |
| 67 | Male | Mild | Mild | Mild | t3 |
| 68 | Male | Mild | Mild | No | t4 |
| 83 | Male | Moderate | Moderate | No | t5 |
| 73 | Male | Mild | Moderate | No | t6 |
| 71 | Female | Mild | Moderate | No | t7 |

Continued on next page

| Age | Gender | Hearing | Vision | Manual Dexterity | Beneficiary Code (g=Germany, i=Ireland, t=Turkey) |
|-----|--------|---------|--------|------------------|-------------------------------------------------|
| 70  | Female | Mild    | Mild   | No               | t8                                              |

## Device Images

Doro PhoneEasy ® 332

Doro Mock-Up created using the framework

Arçelik - Grundig large silver

Arçelik - Grundig large black

Arçelik - Grundig small black

Arçelik - Arçelik Washing Machine Panel 1

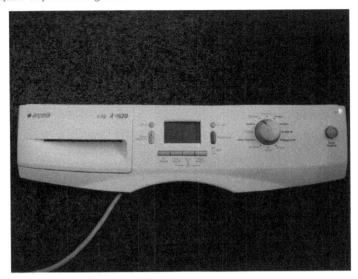

Arçelik - Arçelik Washing Machine Panel 2

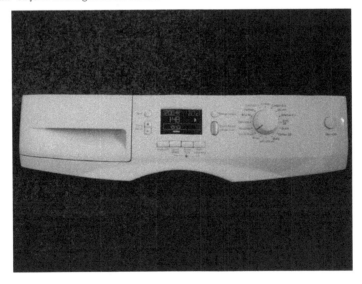

170

## Doro PhoneEasy 332

| Issue | Participants |
|---|---|
| Correctly identified on button | i3, i4, i8, i11, i14, i17, i20, g1, g2, g4, g6, g7, g8, g9, g11, g12, g15, g16, g17, g20 |
| Failed to correctly identify on button at first attempt | i1, i2, i5, i6, i7, i9, i10, i13, i15, i16, i18, i19, g5, g10, g13, g14, g18, g19 |
| Correctly interacted with the on button without assistance | i3, i4, i13, i15, i16, i17, i19, g1, g2, g4, g6, g7, g8, g9, g10, g11, g12, g13, g14, g15, g16, g17, g19, g20 |
| Mistook the "green" button for the on button | i5, i9, i11, i13, i16, g5, g10, g13, g14, g19 |
| Mistook the lock button for the on button | i1, i2, i5, i8, i9, i13, i15, i16, i18 |
| Mistook the scroll (up/down) buttons for the on button | i6, i10, i11, i15 |
| Mistook the flashlight button for the on button | i2, i18 |
| Mistook the flashlight itself for the on button | i13 |
| Mistook the volume buttons for the on button | i17 |
| Failed to correctly interact with on button without assistance | i1, I2, i3, i6, i7, i8, i9, i10, i11, i14, i18, i20, g9 |
| Correctly identified off button without assistance | i1, i2, i4, i5, i8, i10, i13, i14, i15, i16, i17, i19, i20, g1, g2, g4, g5, g6, g7, g8, g9, g10, g11, g12, g13, g14, g15, g16, g17, g18, g19, g20 |
| Correctly interacted with off button without assistance | i1, i2, i4, i5, i8, i10, i13, i15, i16, i17, i19, i20, g1, g2, g4, g5, g6, g7, g8, g9, g10, g11, g12, g13, g14, g15, g16, g17, g18, g19, g20 |
| Failed to correctly identify off button without assistance | i3, i6, i7, i9, i11, i18 |
| Difficulty correctly interacting with off button | i3, i6, i7, i9, i11, i12, i18 |
| Successfully dialled number | i1, i2, i3, i4, i5, i6, i7, i8, i9, i10, i11, i13, i14, i15, i16, i17, i18, i19, i20, g1, g2, g4, g5, g6, g7, g8, g9, g10, g11, g12, g13, g14, g15, g16, g17, g18, g19, g20 |
| Successfully pressed green button to connect call | i1, i2, i4, i5, i6, i7, i8, i9, i10, i11, i13, i14, i15, i16, i17, i18, i19, i20, g1, g2, g4, g5, g6, g7, g8, g9, g10, g11, g12, g13, g14, g15, g16, g17, g18, g19, g20 |

Continued on next page

| Issue | Participants |
|---|---|
| Failed to press green button to connect the call | i3 |
| Made a typing mistake with the numbers | g2, g3, g6, g7, g8, g9, g12, g15, g17 |
| Pressed red button to connect call | i8, g19 |
| Pressing buttons harder than necessary | i11, i14 |
| Pressed two buttons at the same time to connect the call (fingers too large) | i14 |
| Confused by the A (speed dial) key | g10 |
| Successfully identified that a call was coming in | i1, i2, i3, i4, i5, i6, i7, i8, i9, i10, i11, i13, i14, i15, i16, i17, i18, i19, i20, g1, g2, g4, g5, g6, g7, g8, g9, g10, g11, g12, g13, g14, g15, g16, g17, g18, g19, g20 |
| Successfully pressed green button to answer the call | i1, i2, i3, i4, i5, i6, i7, i8, i9, i10, i11, i13, i14, i15, i16, i17, i18, i19, i20, g1, g2, g4, g5, g6, g7, g8, g9, g10, g11, g12, g13, g14, g15, g16, g17, g18, g19, g20 |
| Pressed up and down before "green" button to answer call | i15 |
| Pressed "red" button at first attempt to answer call | g10 |
| Unclear speech due to crackling or feedback | i1, g5 |
| Difficult to hear speech | i2, i7, g7, g15 |
| Does not use text messaging | i9, i10, i19, g2, g5, g6, g7, g8, g9, g13, g14 |
| Failed to successfully type the complete text message | i6, i7, i14, g10, g18, g19 |
| 7/24 assumed the phone was set to predictive text | i1, i2, i3, i13, g10, g18, g20 |
| 17/24 assumed the phone was set to non-predictive text | i4, i5, i8, i11, i15, i16, i17, i18, i20, g1, g4, g11, g12, g15, g16, g17, g19 |
| 18/27 had difficulty with typing double letters in a word. In all cases the beneficiaries pressed the button for the second time too quickly. | i2, i3, i4, i8, i11, i13, i15, i17, i20, g1, g4, g10, g12, g15, g17, g18, g19, g20 |
| Successfully identified text message button | i1, i2, i3, i4, i8, i11, i17, g1, g4, g10, g11, g12, g15, g16, g17, g18, g19, g20 |
| Successfully opened text message | i1, i3, i4, i5, i7, i8, i11, i13, i14, i15, i16, i17, i18, i20, g1, g4, g10, g11, g12, g15, g16, g17, g18, g19, g20 |

Continued on next page

| Issue | Participants |
|---|---|
| Successfully read text message | i1, i3, i4, i5, i7, i8, i11, i13, i14, i15, i16, i17, i18, i20, g1, g4, g10, g11, g12, g15, g16, g17, g18, g19, g20 |
| 6/38 reported that the labelling was too small | i9, i10, i14, g1, g10, g17 |
| 5/38 reported that the keys themselves were too small | i9, i16, g4, g10, g13 |
| 12/38 did not think the buttons were spaced apart enough. | i14, i15, i16, g4, g5, g6, g7, g8, g9, g10, g13, g15 |
| 3/38 did not like the surface shape of the keys reporting that fingers could not easily press the keys without sliding off | i11, i15, g12 |
| 1/38 thought the number keys should be raised more from the surface of the phone | g4 |
| 1/38 reported that the keys were too big | i11 |
| 13/19 did not recognise the A, B and C (speed dial) buttons | i2, i3, i6, i7, i8, i9, i10, i13, i14, i16, i17, i18, i19 |
| 11/19 did not recognise the lock button | i1, i2, i5, i6, i8, i14, i15, i16, i17, i18, i19 |
| 3/19 did not recognise the volume buttons | i3, i4, i6, i7 |
| 2/19 did not recognise the select menu option buttons | i6, i9 |
| 1/19 thought the select menu option buttons were too small | i14 |

## Doro Mock-Up phone developed using the software

| Issue | Participants |
|---|---|
| 2/19 beneficiaries found the phone too wide to comfortably hold. | i1, i20 |
| 1/19 beneficiaries was unable to use the phone one-handed, as desired. | i1 |
| 12/19 beneficiaries did not immediately recognise the on/off button. | i1, i2, i4, i5, i6, i7, i8, i9, i10, i13, i15, i18 |
| One person who successfully identified the "on" button, failed to identify the "off" button. | i19 |
| 7/19 people had to be prompted by the researcher as to where the on button was. | i6, i8, i9, i10, i13, i15, i18 |

Continued on next page

173

| Issue | Participants |
|---|---|
| Once told how to turn the phone on, 9/19 successfully turned the phone off without prompting. | i1, i2, i4, i5, i7, i8, i9, i10, i13 |
| All of the beneficiaries successfully dialled the number. | i1, i2, i3, i4, i5, i6, i7, i8, i9, i10, i11, i13, i14, i15, i16, i17, i18, i19, i20 |
| 18/19 of the beneficiaries successfully pressed the "green" button to connect the call. | i1, i2, i3, i5, i6, i7, i8, i9, i10, i11, i13, i14, i15, i16, i17, i18, i19, i20 |
| 1/19 pressed the "green" button before dialling the number. | i4 |
| 1/19 was unable to use the phone one-handed, as desired. | i1 |
| 8/16 successfully guessed that the envelope button was linked to text messaging. | i2, i3, i4, i8, i13, i16, i17, i18 |
| All 16 successfully read and identified the letters on the keys. | i1, i2, i3, i4, i5, i6, i7, i8, i11, i13, i14, i15, i16, i17, i18, i20 |
| All 16 successfully pressed the correct keys. | i1, i2, i3, i4, i5, i6, i7, i8, i11, i13, i14, i15, i16, i17, i18, i20 |
| All users were happy with the size of the numeric buttons and with the labels on those buttons. | i1, i2, i3, i5, i6, i7, i8, i9, i10, i11, i13, i14, i15, i16, i17, i18, i19, i20 |
| 1/19 user would prefer one-handed use | i1 |
| 2/19 users would prefer less spacing between buttons | i3, i13 |
| For 8/19 beneficiaries, the on/off button was not obvious | i1, i2, i5, i6, i7, i9, i10, i15 |
| 16/19 did not recognise A, B and C buttons | i2, i3, i4, i5, i6, i7, i8, i9, i10, i13, i14, i15, i16, i17, i18, i19 |
| 8/19 did not recognise the volume buttons | i3, i4, i6, i7, i14, i15, i16, i18 |
| 2/19 did not recognise scroll up/down buttons | i15, i18 |

## Grundig Large Silver Remote Control

| Issue | Participants |
|---|---|
| 39/47 beneficiaries successfully identified the on/off button | i1, i2, i7, i8, i9, i11, i12, i13, i14, i15, i16, i17, i18, g1, g2, g4, g5, g6, g7, g8, g9, g10, g11, g12, g13, g14, g15, g16, g17, g19, g20, t1, t2, t3, t4, t5, t6, t7, t8 |

Continued on next page

| Issue | Participants |
|---|---|
| A further three beneficiaries successfully identified the on/off button on their second guess | i5, i10, g18 |
| Five beneficiaries had to be told where the on/off button was | i3, i4, i6, i19, i20 |
| 43/47 beneficiaries expected the on/off button to be at the top of the remote control - either on right or left | i1, i2, i4, i5, i7, i8, i10, i11, i12, i13, i14, i15, i16, i17, i18, i20, g1, g2, g4, g5, g6, g7, g8, g9, g10, g11, g12, g13, g14, g15, g16, g17, g18, g19, g20, t1, t2, t3, t4, t5, t6, t7, t8 |
| Two beneficiaries failed to identify that on and off would be on the same button | i4, i6 |
| All 47 beneficiaries were able to physically press the on/off button | i1, i2, i3, i4, i5, i6, i7, i8, i9, i10, i11, i12, i13, i14, i15, i16, i17, i18, i19, i20, g1, g2, g4, g5, g6, g7, g8, g9, g10, g11, g12, g13, g14, g15, g16, g17, g18, g19, g20, t1, t2, t3, t4, t5, t6, t7, t8 |
| Two beneficiaries reported that it would be better if the button could be bigger | t7, t8 |
| 37/47 beneficiaries successfully identified the volume up/down buttons | i1, i4, i6, i7, i8, i11, i12, i13, i15, i17, i20, g1, g2, g4, g5, g6, g7, g8, g9, g10, g11, g12, g13, g14, g15, g16, g17, g19, g20, t1, t2, t3, t4, t5, t6, t7, t8 |
| Two further beneficiaries identified the correct buttons on their second guess | i14, i16 |
| Eight beneficiaries failed to identify the volume up/down buttons and had to be prompted by the researcher. | i2, i3, i5, i9, i10, i18, i19, g18 |
| All 47 beneficiaries were able to physically press the volume up/down buttons | i1, i2, i3, i4, i5, i6, i7, i8, i9, i10, i11, i12, i13, i14, i15, i16, i17, i18, i19, i20, g1, g2, g4, g5, g6, g7, g8, g9, g10, g11, g12, g13, g14, g15, g16, g17, g18, g19, g20, t1, t2, t3, t4, t5, t6, t7, t8 |
| 46/47 beneficiaries successfully identified buttons | i1, i2, i3, i4, i5, i6, i7, i8, i9, i10, i11, i12, i13, i15, i16, i17, i18, i19, i20, g1, g2, g4, g5, g6, g7, g8, g9, g10, g11, g12, g13, g14, g15, g16, g17, g18, g19, g20, t1, t2, t3, t4, t5, t6, t7, t8 |
| One beneficiary failed to identify the 5-1-7 buttons and had to be prompted by the researcher. | i14 |

Continued on next page

| Issue | Participants |
|---|---|
| All 39 beneficiaries were able to physically press the 5-1-7 buttons | i1, i2, i3, i4, i5, i6, i7, i8, i9, i10, i11, i12, i13, i14, i15, i16, i17, i18, i19, i20, g1, g2, g4, g5, g6, g7, g8, g9, g10, g11, g12, g13, g14, g15, g16, g17, g18, g19, g20 |
| Ten beneficiaries reported difficulty reading the labels | i2, i3, i4, i6, i8, i9, i10, i13, i14, i19 |
| 25/28 beneficiaries successfully identified the location of compartment | i1, i2, i3, i4, i5, i6, i7, i8, i9, i10, i11, i12, i13, i14, i15, i16, i17, i19, i20, t1, t2, t3, t4, t5, t8 |
| 24/28 successfully identified how to open the compartment | i1, i2, i3, i4, i5, i6, i7, i8, i9, i10, i11, i12, i13, i14, i15, i16, i17, i19, i20, t1, t2, t3, t4, t5 |
| Ten had difficulty when opening the compartment | i2, i4, i5, i9, i11, i12, i14, i16, i18, t7 |
| 27/28 successfully identified how to close the compartment | i1, i2, i3, i4, i5, i6, i7, i8, i9, i10, i11, i12, i13, i14, i15, i16, i17, i19, i20, t1, t2, t3, t4, t5, t6, t7, t8 |
| Eleven had difficulty when closing the compartment | i4, i9, i11, i14, i15, i17, i18, i20, t6, t7, t8 |
| Three beneficiary failed to successfully open or close the battery compartment | i18, t7, t8 |
| 39/47 reported a general difficulty when reading the labels | i2, i3, i4, i6, i7, i8, i9, i10, i11, i12, i13, i14, i15, i16, i17, i18, i19, i20, g1, g2, g4, g5, g6, g7, g8, g9, g10, g11, g12, g13, g14, g15, g16, g17, g18, g19, g20, t7, t8 |
| 13/47 specifically reported a difficulty understanding the labels or symbols. These difficulties, however, relate to the buttons that were omitted from the tasks above. | i2, i5, i8, i9, i11, i12, i13, i20, g1, g2, g14, t7, t8 |
| Doesn't like the rocker switch | i15 |

## Grundig Large Black Remote Control

| Issue | Participants |
|---|---|
| 27/47 beneficiaries successfully identified the on/off button at first guess | i1, i2, i7, i8, i9, i11, i12, i13, i14, i15, i16, i17, i18, g1, g2, g4, g6, g8 g12, g15, g16, g19, t3, t4, t5, t6, t8 |
| Two successfully identified the correct button for on only (i4, i5), while one successfully identified it for off only | i6 |

Continued on next page

| Issue | Participants |
|---|---|
| Accordingly, these three beneficiaries failed to recognise that on and off would be on the same button | i4, i5, i6 |
| Nine failed to identify either on or off correctly | i3, i10, i19, i20, t1, t2, t7 |
| 36 of the 39 beneficiaries expected the on/off button to be at the top of the remote control | i1, i2, i4, i5, i7, i8, i10, i11, i12, i13, i14, i15, i16, i17, i18, i20, g1, g2, g4, g5, g6, g7, g8, g9, g10, g11, g12, g13, g14, g15, g16, g17, g18, g19, g20 |
| 42/47 beneficiaries were able to physically press the on/off button | i1, i2, i3, i4, i5, i6, i7, i8, i9, i10, i11, i12, i13, i14, i15, i16, i17, i18, i19, i20, g1, g2, g4, g5, g6, g7, g8, g9, g10, g11, g12, g13, g14, g15, g16, g17, g18, g19, g20, t7, t8 |
| 39/47 of the beneficiaries identified the volume up/down buttons at first glance | i1, i2, i4, i5, i7, i8, i9, i10, i11, i12, i13, i15, i16, i17, i18, i20, g1, g4, g5, g6, g7, g8, g9, g10, g11, g12, g13, g14, g15, g16, g17, g18, t1, t2, t3, t4, t5, t6, t8 |
| Four mistook the P+/- buttons for the volume buttons | i3, i6, i14, i19 |
| All 47 beneficiaries were able to physically press the volume up/down buttons | i1, i2, i3, i4, i5, i6, i7, i8, i9, i10, i11, i12, i13, i14, i15, i16, i17, i18, i19, i20, g1, g2, g4, g5, g6, g7, g8, g9, g10, g11, g12, g13, g14, g15, g16, g17, g18, g19, g20, t1, t2, t3, t4, t5, t6, t7, t8 |
| 42/47 beneficiaries successfully identified the 5-1-7 buttons | i1, i2, i3, i4, i5, i6, i7, i8, i9, i10, i11, i12, i13, i15, i16, i17, i18, i19, i20, g1, g2, g4, g5, g7, g11, g12, g13, g14, g15, g16, g17, g18, t1, t2, t3, t4, t5, t6, t8 |
| All 39 beneficiaries were able to physically press the 5-1-7 buttons | i1, i2, i3, i4, i5, i6, i7, i8, i9, i10, i11, i12, i13, i14, i15, i16, i17, i18, i19, i20, g1, g2, g4, g5, g6, g7, g8, g9, g10, g11, g12, g13, g14, g15, g16, g17, g18, g19, g20 |
| Five beneficiaries were unable to identify how to find channel 517 | g6, g8, g9, g10, t7 |
| One beneficiary declined to carry out the task so the sample size is reduced to 46. | g14 |
| All beneficiaries who attempted the task (46) successfully identified the location of compartment | i1, i2, i3, i4, i5, i6, i7, i8, i9, i10, i11, i12, i13, i14, i15, i16, i17, i18, i19, i20, g1, g2, g4, g5, g6, g7, g8, g9, g10, g11, g12, g13, g15, g16, g17, g18, g19, g20, t1, t2, t3, t4, t5, t6, t7, t8 |

Continued on next page

| Issue | Participants |
|---|---|
| 43/46 successfully identified how to open the compartment. | i1, i2, i3, i4, i5, i6, i7, i8, i9, i10, i11, i12, i13, i14, i15, i16, i17, i19, i20, g1, g2, g4, g5, g6, g7, g8, g9, g10, g11, g12, g13, g15, g16, g17, g18, g19, g20, t1, t2, t3, t4, t5, t8 |
| Three had difficulty when opening the compartment | i1, i5, t7 |
| 45/46 successfully identified how to close the compartment | i1, i2, i3, i4, i5, i6, i7, i8, i9, i10, i11, i12, i13, i14, i15, i16, i17, i19, i20, g1, g2, g4, g5, g6, g7, g8, g9, g10, g11, g12, g13, g15, g16, g17, g18, g19, g20, t1, t2, t3, t4, t5, t6, t7, t8 |
| However 21/46 had difficulty when closing the compartment, specifically with lining up the compartment cover to slide it into place. | i1, i2, i3, i6, i9, i10, i11, i12, i16, i17, i19, i20, g2, g4, g5, g7, g8, g12, g13, t1, t8 |
| Two beneficiaries failed to successfully open or close the battery compartment | i18, t7 |
| 25/47 beneficiaries reported that the smaller buttons on the remote control were too small. It should be noted however that these buttons were not included in the tasks above. | i5, i9, i10, i13, i14, i15, i16, i17, i18, g1, g4, g5, g7, g10, g13, g14, g15, g16, g19, t2, t3, t4, t6, t7, t8 |
| Nine beneficiaries reported that there were too many buttons on the remote control | i11, i14, i15, i16, g1, g2, g13, g18, g19 |

## Small Black Remote Control

| Issue | Participants |
|---|---|
| 45/47 beneficiaries successfully identified the on/off button | i1, i2, i4, i5, i7, i8, i9, i10, i11, i12, i13, i14, i15, i16, i17, i18, i20, g1, g2, g4, g5, g6, g7, g8, g9, g10, g11, g12, g13, g14, g15, g16, g17, g18, g19, g20, t1, t2, t3, t4, t5, t6, t7, t8 |
| One successfully identified the off button only | i6 |
| Two failed to correctly identify either on or off | i3, i19 |
| 45/47 expected the button to be at the top of the remote control | i1, i2, i4, i5, i6, i7, i8, i9, i10, i11, i12, i13, i14, i15, i16, i17, i18, i20, g1, g2, g4, g5, g6, g7, g8, g9, g10, g11, g12, g13, g14, g15, g16, g17, g18, g19, g20, t1, t2, t3, t4, t5, t6, t7, t8 |
| All 47 beneficiaries were able to physically press the on/off button | i1, i2, i3, i4, i5, i6, i7, i8, i9, i10, i11, i12, i13, i14, i15, i16, i17, i18, i19, i20, g1, g2, g4, g5, g6, g7, g8, g9, g10, g11, g12, g13, g14, g15, g16, g17, g18, g19, g20, t1, t2, t3, t4, t5, t6, t7, t8 |
| Two didn't like the feel of the button press | i15, t7 |
| 45/47 beneficiaries successfully identified the volume up/down buttons | i1, i2, i3, i4, i5, i8, i9, i11, i12, i13, i14, i15, i16, i17, i18, i19, i20, g1, g2, g4, g5, g6, g7, g8, g9, g10, g11, g12, g13, g14, g15, g16, g17, g18, g19, g20, t1, t2, t3, t4, t5, t6, t7, t8 |
| Five mistook the up/down buttons for the volume buttons at first | i3, i4, i5, i6, i14 |
| Four mistook the mute button for the volume button at first | i7, i10, i11, i14 |
| Of the nine beneficiaries who failed to identify the buttons at first guess, three failed to correctly identify the volume up/down buttons at all | i6, i7, i10 |
| All 47 beneficiaries were able to physically press the volume up/down buttons | i1, i2, i3, i4, i5, i6, i7, i8, i9, i10, i11, i12, i13, i14, i15, i16, i17, i18, i19, i20, g1, g2, g4, g5, g6, g7, g8, g9, g10, g11, g12, g13, g14, g15, g16, g17, g18, g19, g20, t1, t2, t3, t4, t5, t6, t7, t8 |

Continued on next page

| Issue | Participants |
|---|---|
| 32/47 beneficiaries successfully identified the channel up button | i1, i2, i4, i5, i8, i9, i10, i14, i16, i17, i18, i20, g4, g8, g9, g10, g11, g12, g13, g14, g15, g16, g17, g19, t1, t2, t3, t4, t5, t6, t7, t8 |
| Nine beneficiaries suggested the Menu button as an option | i8, i15, i17, i18, i19, i20, g2, g8, g18 |
| Six beneficiaries were unable to suggest a button that might bring them to channel 517 | i3, i6, i7, i11, i12, i13 |
| All 47 beneficiaries were able to physically press the up button | i1, i2, i3, i4, i5, i6, i7, i8, i9, i10, i11, i12, i13, i14, i15, i16, i17, i18, i19, i20, g1, g2, g4, g5, g6, g7, g8, g9, g10, g11, g12, g13, g14, g15, g16, g17, g18, g19, g20, t1, t2, t3, t4, t5, t6, t7, t8 |
| One beneficiary declined to carry out this task | g2 |
| 43/46 beneficiaries successfully identified the location of compartment | i1, i2, i3, i4, i5, i6, i7, i8, i9, i10, i11, i12, i13, i14, i15, i16, i17, i19, i20, g1, g2, g4, g5, g6, g7, g8, g9, g10, g11, g12, g15, g16, g17, g18, g19, t1, t2, t3, t4, t5, t6, t7 |
| 44/46 beneficiaries successfully identified how to open compartment | i1, i2, i3, i4, i5, i6, i7, i8, i9, i10, i11, i12, i13, i14, i15, i16, i17, i18, i19, i20, g1, g2, g4, g5, g6, g7, g8, g9, g10, g11, g12, g15, g16, g17, g18, g19, t1, t2, t3, t4, t5, t6, t7, t8 |
| Seven had difficulty when opening the compartment | i9, i10, i11, i14, i19, i20, g20, t3 |
| All 46 beneficiaries successfully identified how to close compartment | i1, i2, i3, i4, i5, i6, i7, i8, i9, i10, i11, i12, i13, i14, i15, i16, i17, i18, i19, i20, g1, g4, g5, g6, g7, g8, g9, g10, g11, g12, g13, g14, g15, g16, g17, g18, g19, g20, t1, t2, t3, t4, t5, t6, t7, t8 |
| Four had difficulty when closing the compartment | i3, i9, i10, t4 |
| Issues reported by the beneficiaries (n=22/47) in relation to the look and feel of the keys and controls related to confusion about the functions of certain buttons. Most commonly the buttons that were not tested in the tasks above. | i1, i3, i4, i5, i6, i8, i9, i11, i12, i13, i15, i17, i18, i19, i20, g5, g6, g13, g16, g17, t3, t7 |

Continued on next page

180

| Issue | Participants |
|---|---|
| One beneficiary mentioned the glossy finish on the remote control would get dirty, as there were fingerprints on it | g14 |
| Two beneficiaries reported that buttons were difficult to push | t3, t7 |

## Arçelik Washing Machine Panel 1

| Issue | Participants |
|---|---|
| All beneficiaries successfully identified the on/off button | t1, t2, t3, t4, t5, t6, t7, t8 |
| Two beneficiaries reported that button was hard to hold and push | t3, t7 |
| All beneficiaries successfully identified the set Program A | t1, t2, t3, t4, t5, t6, t7, t8 |
| 6/8 beneficiaries reported that knob is hard to hold and turn around to set Program A | t1, t3, t4, t5, t6, t7 |
| One beneficiary mentioned that knob would be hard to use when hands are wet or soapy | t7 |
| All beneficiaries successfully identified the set Program B | t1, t2, t3, t4, t5, t6, t7, t8 |
| 6/8 beneficiaries reported that knob is hard to hold and turn around to set Program B | t1, t3, t4, t5, t6, t7 |
| All beneficiaries successfully identified the set Program C | t1, t2, t3, t4, t5, t6, t7, t8 |
| 6/8 beneficiaries reported that knob is hard to hold and turn around to set Program C | t1, t3, t4, t5, t6, t7 |
| All beneficiaries had difficulty reading labels | t1, t2, t3, t4, t5, t6, t7, t8 |
| 4/8 beneficiaries reported that it is hard to find and understand programmes | t1, t4, t6, t8 |
| 2/8 beneficiaries reported that there is so many details on the labels, making it confusing | t2, t3 |
| All beneficiaries successfully identified the Main Control panel | t1, t2, t3, t4, t5, t6, t7, t8 |
| 6/8 beneficiaries have mentioned that some of texts are not meaningful and not easy-to-use | t1, t2, t3, t4, t5, t7 |
| One beneficiary reported that it might be better if some text was more colourful or was identified by shapes | t7 |
| All beneficiaries successfully identified the Minor Controls panel | t1, t2, t3, t4, t5, t6, t7, t8 |
| 6/8 beneficiaries reported that some of labels are not easy-to-understand | t2, t3, t4, t5, t6, t7 |

## Arçelik Washing Machine Panel 2

| Issue | Participants |
|---|---|
| All beneficiaries successfully identified the on/off button | t1, t2, t3, t4, t5, t6, t7, t8 |
| Two beneficiaries reported that button is hard to hold and push | t3, t7 |
| All beneficiaries successfully identified the set Program A | t1, t2, t3, t4, t5, t6, t7, t8 |
| 7/8 beneficiaries reported that knob is hard to hold and turn around to set Program A | t1, t2, t3, t4, t5, t6, t7 |
| All beneficiaries successfully identified the set Program B | t1, t2, t3, t4, t5, t6, t7, t8 |
| 7/8 beneficiaries reported that knob is hard to hold and turn around to set Program B | t1, t2, t3, t4, t5, t6, t7 |
| 5/8 beneficiaries reported that knob is too small to hold and control it | t1, t3, t4, t5, t7 |
| All beneficiaries successfully identified the set Program C | t1, t2, t3, t4, t5, t6, t7, t8 |
| 7/8 beneficiaries reported that knob is hard to hold and turn around to set Program C | t1, t2, t3, t4, t5, t6, t7 |
| 5/8 beneficiaries reported that knob is too small to hold and control it | t1, t3, t4, t5, t7 |
| 7/8 beneficiaries have successfully understand the Program Guide | t1, t3, t4, t5, t6, t7, t8 |
| All beneficiaries have some problems to understand some parts of guide | t1, t2, t3, t4, t5, t6, t7, t8 |
| 5/8 beneficiaries reported that it is hard to find and understand programmes | t2, t3, t4, t6, t7 |
| 4/8 beneficiaries reported that text was hard-to-read without glasses | t5, t6, t7, t8 |
| All beneficiaries successfully identified the Main Control panel | t1, t2, t3, t4, t5, t6, t7, t8 |
| 5/8 beneficiaries mentioned that some of the text is not easy to understand | t1, t2, t3, t4, t5 |
| All beneficiaries successfully identified the Minor Controls panel | t1, t2, t3, t4, t5, t6, t7, t8 |
| 4/8 beneficiaries reported that some of labels are not easy to understand | t1, t3, t4, t5 |

www.ingramcontent.com/pod-product-compliance
Lightning Source LLC
LaVergne TN
LVHW042334060326
832902LV00006B/171